SID JAMES

Sid James is one of Cliff Goodwin's four best-selling biographies. He is also the author of *To Be A Lady: The Story of Catherine Cookson*, *When the Wind Changed: The Life and Death of Tony Hancock* and *Evil Spirits: The Life of Oliver Reed*.

Cliff Goodwin was born in London in 1950. He was educated in Slough, Berkshire, and joined the town's weekly newspaper as a trainee journalist in 1968. Since then he has worked in newspapers, magazines, public relations and for the local radio. His coverage of the 1988 Lockerbie air crash earned him a regional press award. In 1993, after 25 years of journalism, he decided to concentrate on full-time writing. He lives in the north-east of England.

D1341535

SID JAMES

A Biography
Cliff Goodwin

This revised and updated edition first published in 2001 by
Virgin Books Ltd
Thames Wharf Studios
Rainville Road
London
W6 9HA

Reprinted 2001, 2002, 2003

First published in hardback in Great Britain in 1995 by Century

First published in paperback in Great Britain in 1996 by
Arrow Books Limited

A catalogue record for this book is available from the British Library.

ISBN 0 7535 0554 1

Typeset by Deltatype Ltd, Birkenhead, Merseyside
Printed and bound in Great Britain by
Mackays of Chatham PLC

'A person is worth more than a book'

Miep Gies

Preface and Acknowledgements

'Comedy is hard work and I'm not really a comedian,' Sid James once admitted. 'I'm an actor who plays comic parts. I need funny people around me to get the best out of myself. I'm more a counter-puncher, a sort of reactor.'

But Sid James was much more. He was unique. Not simply because his professional career – from his 1946 arrival in England to his death on a Sunderland stage in 1976 – lasted just thirty years. Nor that he crammed into that time no less than 457 radio, television and film appearances. It was that, with his battered features, throaty smoker's voice, twinkling eyes and lecherous laugh, he was one of the true British working-class heroes of the 1950s and 60s.

Sid James's enduring ability to make people laugh – never his first acting ambition – remains with us forever. His cult status continues to grow not simply because he was funny and captured the loyalty of a particular generation; more because he repeatedly reinvented himself and was rediscovered by each new generation in turn.

As a comedy actor, Sid James grew with a nation. First on radio and television in 162 *Hancock's Half Hour*s, as a young and energetic chancer. Later as the cheating, sex-mad hero of the *Carry On* films. Finally, in television's *Bless This House*, as a battered and bewildered middle-aged father.

It was Sid James's peculiar achievement to take his place in the British imagination at a time of profound transition: as the austerity of the post-war years gave way to the atomic 50s and finally the superfluous freedom of the 60s. No other actor reflected an audience's own sense of humour so accurately. We were never simply watching Sid James at work. For three decades a nation's ability to enjoy – and mock – its own fallacies and fantasies was hilariously exploited by one man.

Sid James's workload was as exhausting as it was impressive. One hundred and twenty-eight radio appearances, excluding one-off roles in plays and remakes for BBC worldwide transmission; two hundred and five episodes of television comedy, as well as Christmas and other specials, and no less than one hundred and twenty-four recorded film appearances. He starred in several West End musicals and, in later years, toured the world with a succession of sell-out stage comedies.

The time and help I have been given with this biography – both in 1995 when it was first published and this new edition to mark the twenty-fifth anniversary of Sid James's death – have been immense. There is no practical way, therefore, I can thank every single individual.

Those in the entertainment and film industries who gave up their time to remember and talk about Sid James, or who granted permission for the use of photographs or copyright material, deserve a special mention. Sadly, some are no longer with us. They are:

Bernard Cribbins	Jack Douglas
Ray Galton	Miriam Karlin
Dilys Laye	Moira Lister
Olga Lowe	Michael Medwin
Keith Morris	Peggy Mount
Peter Rogers	Alan Simpson
Michael Sullivan	Victor Spinetti
Barbara Windsor	Ronnie Wolfe

There are two people whose patience I have tried more than most. The first is Sarah Berry, my bullying friend and secretary. The second my agent, Jane Judd, who celebrates the dubious honour of having represented me for ten years.

My deepest thanks must, however, go to Reine James not

only for the memories of her father and the photographs she has allowed me to use, but for her inspiration and support.

Permission to use copyright material was kindly granted by the BBC, David and Charles, Methuen, Headline and *Woman* magazine. While every effort has been made to trace all the copyright holders, I apologise for any oversights and to those I may have inadvertently omitted.

Cliff Goodwin, 2001

PROLOGUE

Sid James was a rare bird. He wasn't much of a comedian and he wasn't much of an actor – he was something much more. He always spoke directly to the audience and whatever he did gave a kind of deep feeling to the people watching him.

Frank Muir

He belied his brash image and all the things he looked like. In fact Sid was a very kind man – yes, and chivalrous. That old-fashioned word really applied to him. He cared for all his friends and they cared very much for him.

Hattie Jacques

Monday, 26 April 1976

A knock on Sid James's dressing room door at the Empire Theatre, Sunderland. It opens and a middle-aged man steps into the room. The 7.30 p.m. curtain is fifteen minutes away and Sid is putting the finishing touches to his make-up.

The man shuffles nervously. 'Excuse me, Mr James, could I have your autograph?' he asks. Sid smiles at the image in the brightly lit mirror above the dressing table and continues with his make-up. 'I could come back later if you're too busy.'

Sid turns and waves the man in. On a side table is a pile of photographs. Without getting up Sid slides one from the top, signs and dates it and hands it to his visitor. 'There you are, mate,' he says, 'be my guest. I hope you enjoy the show.'

Off screen he was a very quiet man with lovely manners and very protective towards women. He wouldn't allow

Meanwhile, on stage, Keith Morris settles himself on his
mark in the centre. In the wings, waiting to make her first
entrance, is Audrey Jeans.

It is Morris's second run with *The Mating Season*. The
previous summer he opened the farce during its ten-week
summer season in Blackpool. The play is now in the early
weeks of a full-length provincial tour. Last week Richmond,
Surrey. This week Sunderland. Next week Yarmouth. It is
a punishing schedule and a punishing play. Like all the Sam
Cree plays written especially for Sid James it means he is on
stage for almost the entire performance.

Morris is dressed in a T-shirt and shorts. He can hear the
sound of the opening bars of the Mr Universe cha-cha
music from the auditorium speakers. As the curtain rises he
begins to exercise with a chest expander. Audrey Jean walks
on and delivers the opening line: 'Are you still trying to
build up your chest, Mervyn?'

A few minutes later Morris makes his exit. Standing in
the wings is Sid James. He is sipping whisky from a glass.
'Good evening, Sid,' says Morris. 'How are you settling in?'
Sid had only arrived in the Wearside town that morning.
The rest of the cast and the scenery had moved into the
Empire Theatre on Sunday. The two actors talk. Morris
thinks Sid looks relaxed but tired.

Another person who notices the change in Sid is actress
Olga Lowe. While she and Sid watch the opening minutes

of the play from the wings, they chat and share a joke. Lowe, too, thinks Sid has lost his sparkle. He looks exhausted. His movements are slow and deliberate.

Sid James makes his entrance. He is greeted by applause, which is quickly followed by non-stop laughter. The opening night performance is going well. At exactly 7.45 p.m. Lowe steps on to the stage. She and Sid exchange a couple of lines and Lowe walks upstage to face the audience. Sid is standing behind her.

Lowe continues to deliver her lines. She is suddenly aware that she has not received an answer. Unknown to Lowe, Sid opens his mouth to speak, takes two steps back and lowers himself on to a sofa. He appears to be holding his chest. Lowe glances over her shoulder. Sid's head falls back, his mouth half open, and his eyes roll back in their sockets.

At first Lowe thinks it is a stunt. She ad-libs: 'Oh, come on, Sid, I've come all this way to see you and you treat me like this.' The audience erupts in laughter.

There is obviously something wrong. Lowe continues to ad-lib as she sidles toward the wings. To her horror the laughter continues. One or two people clap.

'For God's sake bring down the curtain,' Lowe hisses at the prompt assistant. The wings are empty. The prompt assistant runs into the darkness to find a stage hand. Lowe goes on ad-libbing and getting laughs.

When the curtain finally falls Sid is still sitting on the sofa. He slumps slowly on to his side.

Sid James was the anchor man of the Carry On *films. He didn't mind what he played, large parts or small parts, so long as he was in them. That's how he felt and that's how we felt. There was always the sense of safety with Sid around.*

Peter Rogers

Mel James, the Empire manager, approaches the star. He can see Sid is not breathing. He pushes his way through the curtain to deliver the classic comedy line: 'Is there a doctor in the house?' It receives the biggest laugh of the night. 'No, no,' he pleads, 'this is serious. Mr James has collapsed.' A man in the front row gets up and the manager waves him to a side door.

It is obvious to the doctor that Sid James has suffered a heart attack. He is told an ambulance is already on its way.

Valerie James, Sid's wife, has been watching the performance from the back of the stalls. She arrives in the wings as Sid is being lifted from the sofa and laid on the stage. Valerie clings to Olga Lowe's arm. 'Oh God, oh God, oh God,' she repeats as she watches the doctor attempting to revive her husband.

Valerie accompanies her husband in the ambulance. The doctor continues to work on Sid during the short drive to Sunderland Royal Infirmary. It is too late.

Sid James was dead.

Part One

'I'm the eternal dirty old man. I'm a car salesman by nature, a jockey by profession, and as far as the birds go . . . cor blimey.'

CHAPTER ONE

His wide-boy attitude to life; his gravel-throated accent; his indignant aggression; his innocent palliness; his rhythmic swagger; his smile; his yak-yak laugh. For millions Sid James was the archetypal Cockney. A real diamond. Nine carat.

'My grandmother was a Cockney seamstress,' he would boast, giving the impression that his own South African birth was nothing more than a step towards his ultimate return to England. In truth, his family's residence in London was itself no more than a respite in a journey which criss-crossed mainland Europe and went on to span most of the globe.

Laurie Cohen – Sid's father – was born in London, the youngest of Rahle and Solomon Cohen's twelve surviving children. Between their Eastern European marriage in the 1850s and their latest son's arrival in late 1870s' London, the couple had produced fifteen offspring.

Solomon was born in 1835 in Polongen, a small coastal village in what was then known as Kurland, later Latvia. The area's main industry was the excavation and fashioning of amber, a yellow fossil resin used to decorate ornaments. By his teens Solomon had moved to Lebo, on the German–Russian border. It was here he married Rahle Davidoff, three years his senior, whose Granada ancestors had fled the Spanish Inquisition to northern Europe.

To escape conscription into the Russian army to fight the British and French in the Crimea, Solomon needed to shed his Russian name and establish a German ancestry. The couple adopted Rahle's grandmother's maiden name – Kahn – and prepared to head west across Europe.

Always intent on reaching London, Rahle and Solomon

Kahn settled for a year or so in Amsterdam. It gave them time to earn enough money to pay for the passage to England. In the late 1850s the couple set foot on British soil and were promptly given yet another name by the fateful hand of a lowly clerk. What little English Rahle possessed she spoke with a thick German accent, an inflection she retained for the whole of her life. The clerk recording the emigrants misheard her pronunciation of Kahn, and henceforth the family were known as Cohen.

Within a year of their arrival Rahle had given birth to Harriet, the first of her fifteen children. More followed in almost annual succession, between 1860 and 1878, with five boys and seven of Rahle's daughters reaching adulthood. Even before the youngest, Laurie, was born, the family had lost touch with some of the older children. One family legend tells the story of how one of Sid's uncles, Rahle's favourite son, went to sea at the age of sixteen. Several years later another Cohen was drinking in a Rhodesian bar. He raised his glass and announced: 'It's my mother's birthday – drinks all round.' The stranger standing next to him confided it was also his mother's birthday and joined the toast. It soon became apparent the men were long-lost brothers. When Solomon died in May 1911 at the age of seventy-six, all twelve of his children were living abroad either in North America or southern Africa.

Between pregnancies, and to ease the financial pressure of supporting her ever-growing family, Rahle earned a little extra by making and mending clothes and selling her crochet work. By the turn of the century the Cohens were living in Horsley Buildings, a cramped cul-de-sac of small houses not far from Sidney Street in the London borough of Stepney-near-Bow. Each dead-end street was known locally as a 'lane'. Rahle and Solomon Cohen's home was at the far end and directly opposite the street entrance.

Not long after the turn of the century Laurie Cohen – whose name was shortened by the family to 'Lou' – met and fell in love with Reine Solomon, the daughter of a musical hall entertainer billed as 'Ma Solomon'. He soon discovered the family's history bore an uncanny resemblance to his own.

Reine's ancestors were Sephardic Jews and considered themselves of a higher order than the refugees from Eastern Europe and Germany. They had originated in Spain and had also fled the peninsula at the time of the Inquisition. Unable to protect them, the Spanish crown had granted them safe passage to Holland, where many settled and thrived. Reine's grandparents were Dutch. The de Wildts lived in the Jewish quarter of nineteenth-century Amsterdam between the Amstel river and Prins Hendrik Kade. They had two daughters, Flora and Karolyn. Despite their parents' objections both daughters married Eastern European Jews who promptly took their new wives off to London.

Karolyn Rosenberg, a placid and homely woman by all accounts, quickly accepted the limitations – and demands – of her new life. Like Rahle Cohen, she too earned extra pennies as a seamstress during a succession of thirteen pregnancies.

Flora Solomon had greater ambitions. Between the birth of her three children – Sonnie, Lily and Reine – she found limited fame as 'Ma Solomon'. Her guttural Dutch accent was still so strong she was forced to abandon her singing career and concentrate on dancing.

During the last quarter of the nineteenth century 'Ma Solomon' was a regular down-bill performer in the music halls in and around London. The atmosphere and bawdy excitement infected her blood as quickly as the crude greasepaint ingrained itself into her skin. Reine, her youngest daughter, was soon addicted.

Just when or how Reine and Lou Cohen decided that their future lay in showbusiness is not clear. It is almost certain the suggestion came from Reine, a fiercely ambitious woman who craved respectability and despised failure. Lou Cohen, with whom she had fallen hopelessly in love, was already an enthusiastic gambler. He took success wherever he found it and was attracted by the potential riches of a stage career. Sometime before 1910 'Ma Solomon' decided to try her luck in South Africa. When the interest of theatre managers there finally came to an end Granny Solomon – as the family knew her – retired to open a theatrical boarding house in Hancock Street in Hillbrow, a suburb perched on one of the many hills that make up Johannesburg.

It was at the instigation of Granny Solomon that her daughter and son-in-law – already earning a living in England as the comedy and dance duo, Reina and Laurie James – decided to emigrate to the newly constituted Union of South Africa. One of their last bookings was at the Royal Standard Music Hall opposite Victoria railway station. Seventy-four years later Sid would step on the same stage of the rebuilt and renamed Victoria Palace theatre. After the couple's cramped rooms in the East End of London and the austerity of a steerage voyage to Cape Town, the Hillbrow house must have appeared almost luxurious.

Most Johannesburg roads were rutted, sandy and untarred. In winter the vicious winds mixed the loose sand from the streets with the dust from the mine dumps to the south of the town. Semi-detached houses were interspersed with superior, single-storey detached homes. Almost all had corrugated, galvanised iron roofs which roared under the beating of the frequent highveld hailstorms.

The couple lost no time in exploring their new surroundings. From Hillbrow they could hear the familiar sound of trams travelling down Rocky Street in the valley below. On the other side of the hill, to the south, they could see – but not recognise – the business centre of Johannesburg, the three- and four-storey buildings contrasting with the gold-coloured slag heaps and the silhouettes of the mine headgear beyond.

Johannesburg was still a frontier town. But the new money was demanding a new, more sophisticated, lifestyle. To Reine's delight, and Granny Solomon's regret, the raucous music hall entertainment was being replaced by the gentler art of vaudeville. Reine and Lou reworked their act and changed their stage name to Potash and Pearl Mutter.

10

And, with Granny Solomon's introductions, found a ready supply of vaudeville bookings at the Orphean and the Standard Theatre in Johannesburg's Rissik Street.

Vaudeville had its parental roots in music hall and variety. But if music hall attracted its share of female patrons, variety was an all-male domain, where the entertainment wavered between crude and vulgar. Together they spawned vaudeville.

In 1894 a Boston showman recognised the need for a new style of family entertainment. His ambition was to create a theatre where families could enjoy good, clean fun. He called it vaudeville, named after Vau de Vire, a region in Normandy renowned for its ballads and homely songs. Vaudeville played in plush, comfortable theatres with carpets instead of sawdust on the floor. Alcohol was banned. As the audiences arrived they were handed leaflets requesting the men to remove their hats and refrain from spitting.

The performers were governed by equally rigid rules. A notice displayed backstage in most vaudeville theatres proclaimed: 'You are hereby warned that your act must be free from vulgarity and suggestiveness in words, costumes and actions . . . and all vulgar, double-meaning and profane words and songs must be cut out of your act before the first performance.' The inclusion of the word 'damn' meant instant dismissal.

By the turn of the century vaudeville was firmly established in England, from where it spread to the colonies. The theatres, many of them purpose-built, also brought with them vast improvements for the performers. Both sides of the house were warm and luxurious. There were usually two or three performances a day, with around eight acts on the bill. These would include animal acts, acrobats, dance teams, one-act plays, comedians and singers. Reina and Laurie Cohen usually took the second spot on the bill, traditionally a duet. Laurie, billed as Lou James, was also an accomplished stand-up comic.

Within a year of their arrival Reine discovered she was

pregnant. She gave birth, in 1911, to a boy. Lou suggested he should be named Maurice after one of his older brothers.

By August 1912, Reine was expecting her second child. This time she was determined the disruption of her career should be kept to a minimum. There had also been gossip – all of which Lou denied – that during Reine's absence from the theatrical circuit Lou had entertained several women performers in his dressing room.

On 8 May 1913, Reine gave birth to a second boy in a back bedroom of Granny Solomon's house in Hancock Street. ('They must have known Tony was coming,' their son quipped many years later. 'There couldn't have been any other reason.') This time the baby was named Sidney Joel Cohen. Once again both forenames were suggested by Lou. Joel was his father's middle name. Sidney came from Sidney Adler, who had married Lou's sister Kate. The couple were now living in Newcastle, Natal. Before the boy was a week old, both names had been replaced by Sollie.

Legend has it that the infant Sollie made his first, albeit unenthusiastic, stage appearance before an audience when he was just a few months old.

'As soon as my mother was able to get up and about my parents were on tour again,' Sid would frequently recall. 'I was in a skip in the wings while my mum and dad were on stage doing their vaudeville act. I was usually bawling, and Mum used to nip off the stage between scenes to finish feeding me.'

During one performance Reine placed her son in a trunk in the wings hoping he would sleep through the act. Sollie had other ideas. Startled by the band and the bright lights the baby decided to exercise his embryonic James voice. Soon the infant found himself flying through the air between his parents' arms to the wild applause of the paying customers. When he grew too large, Lou would carry his son on stage and show him off to the audience.

Sollie was a precocious and confident child. By the age of three he had been enlisted to scatter the sugar on the stage for his parents' sand dance. The following year he was on stage among the action.

Life at Granny Solomon's boarding house was equally exciting. In 1919 the 'family' was joined from England by Flora Solomon's thirty-year-old unmarried niece, Miriam Rosenburg. But young Sollie's favourite visitor was his father's older brother Louis. Already into his forties, Uncle Louis was considered the 'tough egg' of the family, a hard-drinking, hard-living, compulsive gambler who descended on Hancock Street whenever he needed a free meal or somewhere to hide from his creditors. Sollie adored his uncle and, although a confirmed bachelor, Louis in his own way adopted his lively and talkative nephew. It was a bond Sid would never forget yet rarely recall. Many years later Sid admitted it was his uncle and not his father who first introduced him to gambling.

Young Sollie came to depend more and more on the pleasure – and love – he found in the company of his uncle and the motherly attentions of his grandmother. His parents' peripatetic lifestyle meant they were spending weeks, sometimes months, away from Johannesburg. Very occasionally they took Sollie with them, leaving Maurice at home to attend school. Some time before Sollie's fifth birthday Reine and Lou James joined Boswell's touring circus. Sollie was encouraged to join in and would become an unofficial member of the clown troop.

In 1919 Reine and Lou were spotted by a booking agent and offered a tour of Australia. After years of mediocrity it looked as though things were at last about to improve. There was no hesitation – at least not from Reine. The responsibilities of a mother never appeared to cloud her ambition. Sollie and Maurice were to be scooped from the only home they could remember to live with relatives in Natal. To Sollie it was a cruel and treacherous act which shattered his relationship with his parents – and particularly his mother – forever.

* * *

In 1919, Newcastle – like its British counterpart – was a noisy and energetic town at the centre of a spider's web of high-quality coalfields. Surrounded by well-watered, fertile land and rolling green hills, its booming steel mills cast a gritty shadow across the north Natal landscape.

Communication between Johannesburg and Newcastle, to the south-east, was by rail. What roads existed were dusty and bumpy and slow. 'To anyone living in Johannesburg,' recalls one of Sid's cousins, 'Newcastle was looked upon as moving from England to Spain or Italy.'

Ethnic and religious communities congregated as much for protection as companionship. In 1919 there were only four Jewish families living in Newcastle, most related in some way. Sollie and Maurice were deposited in the childless home of his Uncle Abraham and Aunt Esther. Abraham Cohen – always called 'Bob' by the family – was Lou's older brother and a bookmaker. The town's solitary hotel was owned by Sid's namesake, Sidney Adler, and his wife Kate. One of the family guests staying at the time was Adler's brother, Michael, who had been Senior Jewish Chaplain to the British forces during the First World War.

The two boys soon made friends with their cousin Lily Adler, now Lily Mervis. They walked to and from the Government School together and spent much of their playing hours in each other's company.

Sollie soon impressed his cousin with his talents. He could already sing and dance, and play the piano and the ukulele by ear. 'He was a grand boy,' recalls Mervis, 'full of fun and laughter and with a terrific sense of humour.' The older Maurice, she remembers, was 'quieter and more reserved'.

Sollie's life with his immediate family had effectively ended before his seventh birthday. Undoubtedly a favourite with his aunts and uncles, the sudden adventure turned first to a sense of abandonment and then resentment. The separation Reine and Lou had promised would last only a few months dragged on through one year, and then two.

14

When the Australian tour finally ended in 1921 it was Reine alone who arrived to collect her two children.

As the train pulled into Johannesburg station, Sollie soon discovered he was returning to a dramatically different way of life. Granny Solomon's boarding house had moved from Hancock Street to the Joubert Park district. Reine had ended her career on the stage. And Lou, whom Sollie would see only occasionally, was living with other relatives while the couple's divorce took effect.

One evening, soon after his return, eight-year-old Sollie was informed he would be attending Hospital Hill Primary School, where his cousin Joel Cohen was already a pupil. Joel, five months younger than Sollie, was the youngest son of Lou's sister Deborah. To avoid family confusion Joel, soon after his birth, had been dubbed Sidney.

After the disruption of his early years Sollie found the regimentation of school restrictive. While in Newcastle he was frequently punished for talking in class or interrupting lessons with practical jokes. At the end of each infant and primary school year the pupils sat an examination. Sollie consistently achieved the lowest marks. At the age of ten – in Standard Five – each pupil attempted to gain a School Leaving Certificate to allow them officially to finish their primary school education. Those who passed went on to High School. The remainder were enrolled at a Trade School to qualify as bricklayers, joiners and electricians.

'Sid didn't do very well at school,' Joel Cohen recalled many years later. 'He wasn't the brightest of students.'

One classroom incident in Johannesburg changed young Sollie's life for ever. He had arrived at his new school and been given a desk next to his cousin. Before the first lesson began, the teacher, armed with the registration cards on which were printed the boys' real names, asked: 'Which one of you is Sidney?'

Both boys stood up, Sollie because it was his real name and Sidney because that's what everyone called him.

'Which one is Joel?'

Once again both Sollie and Sidney stood up.

15

'OK,' countered the teacher, 'which one of you is Cohen?'

Sollie and Sidney rose a third time.

The teacher thought for a few seconds and then asked which of the two cousins was the older. Sollie raised his hand.

'Right,' announced the teacher pointing at the younger cousin. 'From now on you will be Joel. And Sollie, you will be called Sidney.'

When he returned home that afternoon, 'Sollie' announced his new name and described the classroom confusion to his parents. All right, said Reine Cohen, we'd better change your surname too. When he returned to school the next day, her son informed the teacher that from that morning the world would know him as . . . Sidney James.

CHAPTER TWO

Sid's hatred of school was matched only by his teachers' insistence that he should learn a 'worthwhile trade'. Not surprisingly, Sid had failed his School Leaving Certificate. Separated from his cousin Joel – who went on to qualify as a surgeon – he was allocated a place at a nearby Trade School and told that his only hope of earning a living would be to qualify as an electrician. Sid had other ideas. During one practical lesson he deliberately mis-wired a household circuit. When the power was switched on the cables burst into flames and the fusebox exploded. The incident did not produce the hoped-for expulsion, but Sid's attendances at school grew less and less. 'I think he more or less dropped out,' recalls Joel Cohen.

Many years later, Sid would retell an edited version of the incident as part of a series of alleged teenage travels whilst attempting to earn a living in Depression-hit South Africa. In it, Sid had signed on as an apprentice electrician. Just why he was helping to re-wire a house after only three days is uncertain but, as he told it, the fusebox sparks were so fierce they set the wooden house alight.

Sid's manipulation of the truth was not confined to the classroom of his Hospital Hill Trade School. His 'education' – which in truth lasted no more than eight years – ranged, according to him, from attending a primary school in the exclusive Johannesburg suburb of Yoeville to studying at various colleges. Two of these that Sid often named are Grey College in Bloemfontein and Houghton College, both far beyond Sid's academic ability.

Confronted by her son's truancy and his growing rebelliousness, Reine turned once again to the family. Not long after his twelfth birthday Sid found himself on his way back to Aunt Esther and Uncle Abraham. The family break-up – this time with no hope of eventual reunion – was painful and deep, and seems to have left Sid with a mistrust of both women and emotional relationships for the rest of his life. Sid felt his mother no longer loved him. It was a classic psychological set-up. The loss of his mother left him with what psychoanalysts describe as a 'failure of transference'. As he grew older Sid was unwilling – indeed, unable – to transfer the love a boy feels for his mother to any other woman. As an 'orphan' in Newcastle Sid was spoiled, but spoiled without the benefit of human affection.

The result of this crisis was immediate yet lifelong. Again, Sid's was a classic reaction. He devoted much of his energies to remodelling the unhappy and unsatisfactory real world into a parallel world of invention and personal propaganda. Sid also felt compelled to wield power, at least until he reached his forties, particularly towards women, as an expression of his ego. Women, he evidently grew to believe, were there to satisfy his libido. Any attempt to control or shape his life, as Reine had done, would be met with fierce and violent jealousy.

For a few years at least Sid was under the controlling influence of his Newcastle relatives. He returned to secondary school there and renewed his friendship with his cousin Lily Adler.

The approach of Sid's thirteenth birthday in 1926 brought with it a further problem for the town's Jewish community. Traditionally Sid should have celebrated his barmitzvah in a synagogue. With a shortage of permanent Jewish families in Newcastle and no synagogue, it was decided he should have a special party instead.

An elderly man, recently arrived from Lithuania, was recruited to teach Sid a few prayers. These Sid recited before his thirteenth birthday party got under way.

One Jewish family who attended the event were Max and Sarah Kahanovitz. They had arrived in Newcastle the

year before with their nine-month-old son. Max Kahanovitz had decided to move from Johannesburg after being
offered the chance to buy the coal town's bankrupt Walsh
and Ryder department store. Sarah Kahanovitz remembers Abraham Cohen, with whom Sid was staying, as a
'stocky, jovial man', with an equally adipose wife. After
school and at weekends Sid would be given jobs at the
store.

By 1928 Reine and her eldest son were living at Yoeville, a
middle-class Johannesburg suburb of bungalows and semi-
detached houses. It was time, she thought, to bring Sid back
into the family. When the Newcastle train pulled into
Johannesburg station and Sid stepped down, Reine was
surprised and impressed by the change in her son. In three
years Sid had evolved from an impish and cheeky young boy
into a nervously confident teenager, brash and bold in the
company of his male peers.

Reine had enrolled her son at a Yoeville Trade School, a
situation Sid soon accepted when he discovered the masters
shared his love of football. Within days of his arrival Sid was
selected for the school team and invited to play in the local
Sunday league.

The weekend games were played on Yoeville Football
Ground, about half a mile from Sid's home. Every few
minutes a tram would clank and clatter past on its way down
to the city centre or up to the Observatory Heights
terminus. His football team colours were blue and white.
Sid, as goalie, was allowed to wear a traditional goalkeeper's
roll-neck jersey.

Sid's Sunday morning acquaintance with fellow team
member Boris Wilson – later to become a member of
parliament for Johannesburg – was a direct result of their
team's impressive performance. While the rest of the
players kept the action at the far end of the pitch, Wilson, as
a full back, had ample time to chat with Sid in goal.

'I will always remember him as an energetic goalie,'
recalls Wilson. 'We would stand around kicking the grass

and chatting. He was one of a bunch of lads who had made their names at school for being jokers and comedians. Every week he would tell me some new jokes or a funny story.'

Two or three times a year Sid and Maurice would spend their holidays with family friends in Halebron in the Orange Free State. It was during one of these holidays, in 1929, that Sid found himself in demand as an actor. Pretty soon he realised he possessed another quality – sex appeal.

Sid's first performance as an actor took place not on stage but in the back garden of a dorp town house. Living in the house were three sisters, the eldest in her mid-teens and the youngest about five years old. From the first visit all three girls fell hopelessly and childishly in love with Sid. 'He was the most handsome, beautiful creature,' recalls the youngest of his admirers. 'His hair was brown and curly with golden highlights and he had the most beautiful green-grey eyes, with lovely long black eyelashes.'

The weekly football game and Sid's love of sports had developed his muscles and kept his skin clear and healthy. The furrowed forehead and wrinkled face – a feature of all the Cohen men – would come later. So too would the pock-marked and scarred cheeks and chin Sid would blame on malfunctioning sweat glands, but which were actually the result of nervous acne. In 1929 he was simply a shy sixteen year old 'with laughing eyes and an immense sense of humour'.

The oldest daughter regularly wrote and produced adaptations of fairy stories and local legends. The plays were performed in the open and friends and relatives not taking part would sit on the grass or an assortment of chairs. This summer, no doubt as a reflection of his growing charisma, Sid was given the part of the handsome Prince Charming in *Sleeping Beauty*.

The rehearsals lasted a few sunny afternoons. When the production started Sid emerged in his makeshift finery trying his best not to play the fool. Around his shoulders was a blue satin and taffeta cloak borrowed from the girls' mother; his trousers had been tied at the knees and tucked into his socks. Sid's princess wore a full-length dress and lay on a commandeered settee awaiting her saviour's kiss. 'He was so shy he blushed terribly,' recalls a member of that small audience. 'It took a lot of cheering for him to actually kiss her.'

If, in the summer of 1929, Sid felt clumsy and awkward in the presence of girls it would soon wear off. He was already outshining Maurice who, despite his darker hair and 'romantic olive-tinted skin', never attracted the opposite sex in quite the same way. Many years later Sid would boast how he had lost his virginity to 'an older woman' before his seventeenth birthday. The story may, or may not, be true, but within a few years Sid had certainly discovered a need – for sex.

Of her two sons Reine still saw Sidney as the problem child. Unlike Maurice, who had already found himself a permanent career in wholesaling, Sid was poorly educated and unmotivated. Worse still, at seventeen, he was already showing signs of his father's irresponsibility and deceit.

Sid would skulk around the hairdressing salon Reine had opened and ran with her brother and sister, and, when he was ordered out, scuff around the streets on the pretence of looking for work. He would, however, never fail to return to the Yoeville house for meals or to sleep. Out among his friends Sid took to boasting about how he had travelled to Durban and Cape Town to earn a living loading ships and trimming coal.

One real job, on which Sid built yet another adult fantasy, was as a diamond sorter. In 1960 he told BBC listeners: 'When I was a youngster I used to do a lot of diamond digging. For ten days, or a couple of weeks, I would be living on my own digging diamonds.' He never explained exactly when this was or why his mother or proto-parents in Newcastle allowed a teenager – who should have been at school – to disappear into the wilderness. Sid elevated this brief sorting job, which many of his contemporaries recall,

21

to that of a highly skilled diamond polisher. He did, however, acquire at least a working appreciation of diamonds and their value. In later years he became an astute collector of uncut diamonds.

In 1930 Reine James issued her son with an ultimatum – join the family business and train as a hairdresser or get out. The next day Sid began work at the Marie Tudor salon.

To his surprise Sid discovered an unexpected aptitude for hairdressing. 'Sid was a born showman,' recalls one of his early colleagues, 'and he soon realised that being a good hairdresser is as much about being a showman as it is about cutting and styling hair.' He had also discovered the difference between wanting to be a man in a man's world and – far more important to Sid – being a man in a woman's world.

Sid found himself in a highly privileged and pampered position. Under his uncle Sonnie Solomon's tutelage he made rapid progress. Within twelve months he was cutting and styling hair. At last he was allowed to attend to Sonnie's more treasured customers, among them the attractive eighteen-year-old daughter of one of Johannesburg's most respectable Jewish families. Her name was Toots Delmont.

Joseph Delmont took an immediate and, as it turned out, justifiable dislike to his youngest daughter's new boyfriend. He sensed in this brash young man a will to succeed and a ruthlessness not far removed from his own. 'That boy will hurt or be hurt,' he was once overheard to say.

Joseph Delmont, a birth-right Cockney, had travelled to southern Africa from England in the 1870s with Cecil Rhodes. Fifty years later he was one of the wealthiest businessmen in Johannesburg. Even into his early sixties he was tall and rugged and possessed piercing blue eyes. He was also an ardent royalist. The walls of his office and the mantelshelf of his Johannesburg home were lined with photographs and paintings of the British royal family. All four of his children were born during the family's biennial visits to London. When the infants returned to South Africa they were always accompanied by an English nanny.

It was one of these English nannies who nicknamed the youngest Delmont daughter 'Toots'. Berthe Sadie Delmont was born in 1912. By the age of two she was universally known as Toots and her real name had slipped into obscurity, a family tradition designed to gently rid the children of their father's liking for exotic names. The eldest son, Alexander, became Alec; Alexandra Rebecca became Bex, and Abigail was nicknamed Eva. Delmont's Britishness – he had earned his fortune exploiting the diamond fields in that part of the Empire – hid his true ancestry. When his forefathers had joined the exodus from Spain they were called Delmonte. Once in England the final 'e' had first fallen silent and then been dropped altogether.

After selling the majority of his diamond interests to De Beers and Anglo–American, Joe Delmont discovered an equally lucrative source of income. By 1930, just as diamond prices slumped with the collapse of the American market, Delmont was sustaining his wealth with a chain of Tattersalls bookmakers across the Union.

All of Delmont's children had grown up in the family house in the smart Jewish suburb of Doornfontein, the Brooklyn of Johannesburg. When Toots was approaching her teens Delmont bought a new home in Francis Street, Yoeville, for his daughters. Large and imposing and painted brilliant white, the house was one of the largest in the suburb. The age difference between the Delmont girls – Bex was six years older and married when Toots first met Sid – meant three separate groups of friends would often descend on the Francis Street house at the same time.

Like most wealthy families where much money had been made and continued to be earned, there was a benevolent nonchalance towards large amounts of cash. Bex, Eva and Toots were undeniably the richest among their group of friends, most of whom came from hard-working but poor families. As the Depression worsened, some of Bex's friends

23

received regular meals in the kitchen of the Francis Street house. There was also the occasional cash hand-out.

Late on Saturday afternoons, when the Tattersalls offices had closed, the managers would deliver the takings to their boss's home. The money arrived in brown paper bags and was tipped on to the large kitchen table. Whichever group of friends happened to be in the house at the time was given the task of sorting and counting the mountain of crumpled notes and coins. Anyone particularly down on their luck that week was slipped a pound or two by Bex or Eva. Joe Delmont protested about the practice but did nothing to halt it.

Toots began to take up more and more of Sid's time and attention. Her musical training – all the Delmont girls had received piano lessons – rekindled in Sid a childhood enjoyment of performing, although at this time his interest lay in music and dance rather than acting. The pair also shared a passion for the Charleston and jazz. Late-night dances at Johannesburg's Carlton Hotel or the Jewish Guild turned into late mornings at the salon. Sonnie mumbled his disapproval but secretly envied his nephew's membership of the flapper set. When Sid, almost casually, let slip his intention of marrying Toots his mother exploded in a fit of frustration and anger. Reine, ambitious yet practical, considered her son too young and unsettled for marriage. Sid felt betrayed at not receiving his mother's support.

Minor irritations escalated into arguments and days of silence. Customers at Marie Tudor began to sense Sid's unhappiness. After one particularly bitter row Sid stormed out and quit. His reputation as a hairdresser, however, was made. Within days he was offered a job at Woolf's hairdressing saloon, only two blocks away. But that wasn't far enough for Sid. He began scanning the Orange Free State newspapers for a salon vacancy out of his mother's reach.

Sid was not yet nineteen. He arrived in Kroonstad in early 1932. It was not what he expected. Kroonstad was open and sprawling, situated a little more than a hundred miles south-west of Johannesburg. Its 50,000 residents qualified it as a town, but in reality it was a scattered farming village held together by a railway junction and a few dusty streets. Each week, with their cattle in the back of their trucks and cars, the farmers would drive to the Kroonstad auction and railhead. Their wives would shop or drink tea or have their hair curled or permed in the town's only hairdressing salon. News of Sid's arrival spread fast. His skill as a hairdresser and his non-stop charm and chatter had the same effect on the females of Kroonstad as if their husbands had sprinkled sugar into their glasses of flat beer.

On one occasion Sid was cutting a woman's hair when he accidentally nicked her earlobe. Unaware of what was happening the woman was still laughing at one of Sid's jokes when he arrived back from the chemist next door with something to staunch the bleeding. Sid hid the woman's injured ear by leaving her hair a fraction longer on that side. When the woman complained about her lop-sided hairstyle Sid convinced her that 'that's how everyone is wearing it in Johannesburg'.

The salon was situated on the main street. Not far away was an optician's run by an upright and 'Victorian' Englishman called Hearn. Old man Hearn's three elder daughters – Claire, Sally and Hanna – were all born in England. As his children grew, Hearn developed an irrational and overpowering fear they might contract tuberculosis. The only sure prevention, he had reasoned, was plenty of sunshine. Soon after the family's arrival in South Africa the fourth Hearn girl, Jacqueline, was born.

Not long after Sid moved to Kroonstad he decided to change his lodgings. He was offered a room in the Hearn house. 'Sid kept everyone alive,' remembers Sally Franks (née Hearn). 'He dined with us quite often and he was always gay and happy and full of jokes.'

It soon became obvious from the dinner table conversations that Sid was unhappy as a hairdresser. 'He hated it,' adds Hanna Obert (née Hearn). 'He absolutely loathed

25

working in the salon. He only had two things he would talk about and that was the theatre, and turning professional and earning lots and lots of money.'

Sid first attempted to earn more money by opening a dance school. To relieve his boredom, Sid turned to sex. There was never a shortage of patrons for both. He hired a large hall at the back of a Kroonstad restaurant. He would play records and teach ballroom dancing. When he was happy he would show off with an impromptu display of tap-dancing or soft-shoe shuffle. His favourite among the Hearn girls was Sally, already an attractive and confident teenager, whom Sid recruited as his dance partner. Like his appoint-ment book at the salon, there were few vacant places at Sid's dance school.

Sid introduced Toots as his fiancée. She made an immediate and lasting impression on the Hearn family, who remember her as a slender person with dark hair – 'with great charm and always delightful to be with'. But when Toots was safely back in Johannesburg Sid continued with his plan to seduce the wives and daughters of Kroonstad – frequently making them pay for the privilege.

One spectacularly successful ploy involved a 'revolutio-nary' new method of ice massage. Sid claimed to have been taught how to use ice to beautify and revive the skin during his training in Johannesburg. The after-hours sessions took place in a screened cubicle at the salon. Sid began by asking the women to strip naked and lie on a treatment couch. He would then use lumps of ice to gently massage their necks and breasts, progressing inevitably to other parts of the body.

When Sid started to get bored with his salon sex sessions he decided to add a little spice to the seductions – by inviting his friends to watch. From a window high in the wall of the cubicle, the older Hearn girls and their friends attempted to stifle their giggles or gawped in silent horror at Sid's exploits. 'A lot of us got our first serious sex lesson from watching Sid,' one admitted.

All this was a safe distance from Reine James. All she

and her brother, Sonnie, were receiving were reports – both first hand and through Toots – of Sid's success as a hairdresser.

By late 1934 though, Sid was once again showing signs of restlessness. He wanted to return to Johannesburg, this time on his own terms.

Mina Stuart looked up at the stone frontage of the Rissik Street department store before plunging through the revolving door. On the second floor, the twenty-eight-year-old Canadian found the Marie Tudor hairdressing salon. While Stuart waited for the manager to appear she took the chance to look around.

The salon was a long, narrow room. To the left were a series of booths, each with its own sink and mirror and chair, and each separated from its neighbour by a frosted glass screen. Stuart could see the backs of half a dozen stylists working on their clients. A young man, dressed in a white coat, appeared from a side door and smiled at her. His hair was dark and wavy and his green eyes reflected the bright lights. Stuart put him at no more than twenty-four or twenty-five years old.

A few minutes later Sonnie Solomon ushered her into an office. Stuart explained she had come to South Africa the year before from Canada. She had two young boys and her husband's £12 a month as a mining engineer was not enough to support the family. She needed a job and she wanted to train as a hairdresser.

'So why have you come to me?' Sonnie asked.

'Because you have the most famous salon in Johannesburg,' Stuart replied.

On the morning Stuart reported for work Sonnie introduced her to the 'charming young man' she had briefly seen before her interview. His name, Stuart learned, was Sidney James.

'There were several trainees,' recalls Stuart, 'and I was probably the oldest. I was even older than Sid. But he was very kind and patient and literally taught me everything he knew about hairdressing.'

Sid and Toots began making plans for their wedding. This time there were no longer any objections from Reine. Yet Sid was far from welcome in the Francis Street house.

A future relative of the Delmonts distilled the family's feelings at the time. 'I think Sid pursued Toots,' explained Joy Kaplan. 'It was as simple and as ruthless as that. She was a rich girl who came from a rich family, a prominent family, and that suited Sid.'

To her sisters and female friends there was no doubt Toots was deeply and blindly in love with Sid – 'She was potty about him.' Sid, too, was obsessed. It became increasingly apparent that the challenge of marrying Toots far outweighed any question of love or the need to make his future wife happy. In so many ways they were already growing apart.

'Toots was a kind, shy girl, but she was no shrinking violet,' recalls Kaplan. 'The deeper she fell for Sid the more possessive and manipulative he became.' Toots regarded warnings about Sid's increasing jealousy as misguided and misplaced.

'You could sense his suspicion whenever you met them together,' added a contemporary. 'You got the feeling that if you physically got too close to Toots or said something Sid considered overly friendly he would order you outside.'

Sid's jealousy could be both irrational and violent. In 1933, as Toots's twenty-first birthday approached, an old friend of the family who had lived with the Delmonts first at Doornfontein and then in the Francis Street house gave Toots a pinkie ring as a present. The middle-aged man was called Freddie and was gentle and charming. Sid hated him. When Toots showed Sid the ring he ripped it from her finger, hurled it to the ground, and stamped on it until the ring shattered.

Sid's insecurity stemmed from his fear of losing 'ultimate

control' over Toots. She had steadfastly refused to be seduced. Toots became an obsession.

'His temper was as great as his humour,' testifies Kaplan, 'which was not unusual in someone so dynamic. But he had that charm and charisma which allowed him, even then, to get whatever he wanted.'

CHAPTER THREE

Faced with his daughter's determination – a family trait he secretly admired – Joe Delmont finally accepted the inevitable.

On 12 August 1936, Sidney James married Berthe Delmont at Johannesburg Central Register Office. The bride and groom were recorded as being of the European 'population group'. Both ages were given as twenty-four. A mistake: three months earlier Sid had celebrated his twenty-third birthday. The reception was held at the Carlton Hotel on Johannesburg's Kirk Street, only a few hundred yards from where Sid worked.

From the first time he saw Toots at the age of eighteen Sid had been determined to marry her. On their first real date he had even told her so – not as a proposal, as a prediction. For Sid the chase was finally over. It was a triumph which heralded not only a beautiful wife, but also respectability and recognition from some of the wealthiest and most established families in South Africa.

Among the guests at the wedding were the Hearn family, who had arrived in Johannesburg not long after their Kroonstad lodger. Faced with the demands of feeding three older daughters and a young child, old man Hearn had decided it was time for a move to the big city. He opened an optician's shop in Kirk Street, directly opposite the Carlton Hotel, and soon expanded into selling cameras and photographic equipment, a venture which proved far more profitable than dispensing glasses. Not to be outdone, his wife opened a nearby store selling instruments and sheet music. And all four Hearn girls renewed their friendship with Toots.

Reine James had already left the family hairdressing salon

to open a high-class clothes shop with her sister, Lily. Their new premises were in the Shepherd and Barker Building. Within weeks Sonnie was taken ill and ordered to retire by his doctor, which left Sid managing the salon for his absent relatives.

Sid began voicing louder and louder his intention of pursuing an acting career. The thought of his over-confident son-in-law departing for England was a possibility Joe Delmont was prepared to live with. The idea of his favourite daughter leaving the protective wing of the family to survive on the precarious wages of an unknown, and so far untried, actor was another matter. One evening soon after their wedding Delmont announced he was buying Sid his own salon. He veiled the offer as a 'belated wedding present'. Everyone in the Delmont family knew it was an attempt to curb Sid's roving instinct.

Joe Delmont never did things by halves. The salon he purchased for his son-in-law was situated in the basement of the Carlton Hotel, then regarded as 'the' hotel in South Africa.

The Carlton Hotel was owned by I. W. Shlesinger, a friend of Joe Delmont. It occupied an entire city block. Built of stone and marble, the ground floor consisted of shops with the three-storey hotel above. The post-depression Carlton was populated by emigrant Jewish stock and old St Petersburg finery. Its public and private rooms were palatial, and its reputation ensured the constant presence of visiting royalty. Sid was already a regular visitor at the hotel. One self-promoting trick he frequently employed when drinking at the hotel was to have himself paged by the bell-boy. Sid would allow the uniformed teenager to tour the bars and lounges several times calling out, 'Mr Sidney James. Message for Mr Sidney James', before standing up and announcing, 'Over here, I'm Sidney James.'

Sid moved into the hotel hairdressing salon and promptly renamed it Maison Renée. He agreed to retain some of the staff employed by the previous owner and persuaded several of his former colleagues to transfer to the plusher surroundings of the Carlton. By 1940 Sid was employing more than thirty stylists and beauticians.

One of several hairdressers who owed their careers to Sid was Rossella Goldberg, now Porter. 'He impressed me immediately with his great charm, friendliness and kindness,' she recalls. One of the first lessons Sid taught his youngest junior was how to pour whisky into a china cup. Like all new trainees Porter was never allowed anywhere near a head of hair. Her duties included sweeping the floor, fetching pins and curlers for the other stylists and serving tea or coffee to the clients. At least four or five times each day Sid would lean back beyond the line of cubicles and call out: 'Rosie, bring me my milk.' Porter would duly arrive with a cup and Sid would down the liquid in one go, shudder, and confess to his client: 'Ugh, how I hate milk.'

As in later years, Sid's attitude to a fellow human being was rarely swayed by a title or rank. It was part of his charm. Maison Renée clients who demanded the exclusive attention of the owner were rarely shown deferential treatment.

Sid was attending one titled English woman when a client two chairs down called out: 'Do you play golf, Mr James?' Sid admitted he did.

'What's your handicap?' the lady enquired, looking into the mirror and up at Sid.

'Boils, pimples, blackheads and piles,' said Sid. 'What's yours?' Sid could feel his English client giggling beneath his hands. A week later they were playing the first of what became a regular round of golf.

Sid had been introduced to betting by his Uncle Louis. Now he was related to the owner of a chain of bookmakers. Gambling, to Sid, was as obsessive – and enjoyable – as sex. He once claimed that watching his horse or dog win was 'better than having an orgasm'.

Johannesburg sported two race courses, one at Auckland Park, the other at Turffontein. Sid was a regular visitor to both. On work days he would place his off-course bets at the Delmont-owned Tattersalls or, out of mischief, make use of one of the rival and illegal 'bucket shops'. To help finance his betting Sid devised an ingenious scheme. He initially borrowed £5 from Sonnie Solomon. When his uncle demanded the money back, one of the hairdressers at the salon was despatched to Dave Marais, a friend of Sid's who ran a nearby health studio. Marais was persuaded to lend Sid £6. The runner delivered a fiver direct to Sonnie, and the remaining pound gave Sid another stake. When Marais called in his debt Sonnie was asked for £7 . . . and so the scam continued. On the rare occasions Sid produced a winner he would settle the debt and start from square one.

Years later Sid would employ a modified version of the scheme to mollify irate bookmakers and extract money from his friends and colleagues. The only difference was that, by then, he had added three noughts.

One of the most popular semi-professional dance bands in late 1930s Johannesburg was Harold Gordon and his Music.

Harold Gordon, a saxophonist with more enthusiasm than musical talent, had secured a regular round of bookings at Johannesburg weddings and barmitzvahs and at the occasional race course meeting. Vacant weekends were filled with community and school hall dances.

The band's piano player was a thin-faced young man called Harry Rabinowitz. Gordon had recruited him on the spur of the moment after hearing piano music coming from the Hillbrow house where Rabinowitz lived. Another member was a short, dapper man in his mid-twenties called Maurice Cohen.

Sid, recently married to Toots, soon discovered the band's lunchtime rehearsals and evening gigs were a rich hunting ground for new women. He would stand in a corner to one side of the stage. To attract attention he would tap-dance or hoof his way through a number. It seldom failed to spark some kind of reaction, recalls Rabinowitz. 'Sometimes it provoked fights and sometimes it provoked romance.'

Marriage – Sid's marriage – was never mentioned. Toots

was a part of Sid's life which floated, unspoken, somewhere out of sight.

'He was always a ladies' man,' adds Rabinowitz. 'When Sid came to our rehearsals or when we would have a drink afterwards he was always on about some woman or other, or some woman would be on about him. There never was a week when Sid was short of females in his life.'

What impressed Rabinowitz more was Sid's impeccable taste in jazz and dance music and his ability to translate almost any tune into a magical and magnetic body language. Rabinowitz explains: 'Sid just heard a tempo and the feet started to move. He knew by instinct what to do to a certain piece of music: hands, legs, smile, face, eyebrows – he just knew.'

Never a handsome man by conventional standards, Sid's confident smile easily made up for his scarred face and receding hairline. In his late teens Sid had shown the first signs of a lifetime's propensity to acne. Untreated, the cysts had left his skin mottled and irregular, 'like a tangerine skin'. It did not affect his confidence.

Confidence was something Sid was never short of. Not long after their own marriage Sid and Toots attended Eva Delmont's wedding. One photograph shows the bride and groom and guests standing rigidly to attention. In the back row is Sid, grinning broadly and with his head resting theatrically on his hand. 'Sid had immense self-confidence,' recalls one family guest. 'You sensed that this man knew he was on a personal journey.'

The picture, when he saw it, infuriated Joe Delmont. It was a slap in the face. An insult. The patriarch had already used his influence and money to save Sid – and he was about to do the same a second time.

By the end of October 1936 – just eighty days after their marriage – Toots discovered the first awful truth: she had been sharing her husband with another woman. Toots bolted for the Francis Street house.

Joe Delmont confronted Sid, who promptly confessed. Throughout the final days of his engagement and the first

34

weeks of his marriage Sid had cheated on Toots. Sid's lover, a fellow hairdresser, was now pregnant and intent on retribution. Delmont, for his daughter's sake if nothing else, took over. The woman was approached and offered a substantial sum of money. There were two conditions: that she leave South Africa and that she never disclose the truth. Sid was told his affair 'had been buried', and Toots returned to her husband.

By February the following year Sid was embroiled in a second relationship, this time with a stylist he had approached to join the staff of the newly opened Maison Renée. She, too, was now pregnant. Aware of her predecessor's fate, there was more than a hint of blackmail about the woman's demand for financial support. This time it was Sid who approached Joe Delmont. Once again the businessman provided the hush-money and shipped his son-in-law's lover out of the country.

There were undoubtedly more affairs and more illegitimate offspring. Joy Kaplan's view: 'Sid was totally immoral. The man was incorrigible and his libido was stupendous. He simply could not help himself.'

A month later Toots informed her husband she was expecting their first child. Sid was 'furious'. In an act of supreme hypocrisy Sid accused his wife of 'betraying' him; of trying to control his life; of stopping him improving himself. The pregnancy, he ranted, was a 'Delmont plot' to end his acting career. Sid shouted and slammed doors and threw things. Finally he lashed out at Toots.

Sid effectively turned his back on the child. Elizabeth James was born in December 1937. Sid, though still living with Toots, took very little interest in either the pregnancy or the birth. During her confinement, Toots took up knitting. She produced bootees, blankets and cardigans – an occupation Sid considered both pointless and demeaning for the daughter of a wealthy family. They seldom went out together. Sid seldom arrived home before midnight.

* * *

Sid became aware of the reputation of the Johannesburg Repertory Players. They were as close to a professional company as Johannesburg possessed. When he joined, in the summer of 1937, Sid was told he was too late to be auditioned for a part in the October production of Ivor Novello's *Fresh Fields*. He began to attend the Sunday evening part reading and lecture sessions at the Carlton Hotel. Just before Christmas he was offered a small part in *Double Error* by Lee Thompson. A three-day run at the Library Theatre had already been booked for the end of February.

Maison Renée, meanwhile, was a success. Business, like its owner's theatrical experience, was increasing week by week. In 1938 the Rep's annual subscription was raised to £1 11s 6d. It was a sum Sid could easily afford, even with a wife and baby to support. Other unpaid parts followed in *They Walk Alone* by Max Catto and Emlyn Williams's *The Corn Is Green*. The following year, at the age of twenty-six, Sid James received his first fee as a professional actor – on radio.

Through his connections at the Johannesburg Rep, Sid had been offered a part in a new series of children's programmes being planned by the South African Broad-casting Corporation. When he arrived at the studios for the first rehearsal Sid found he had been partnered with a fifteen-year-old schoolgirl called Moira Lister.

Each thirty-minute programme included a selection of music and dramatised stories. It was a new experience both for the teenager and her co-star. Although Sid was less than a year away from giving the most talented acting perfor-mance of his career – both as an amateur and a professional – Lister, not yet sixteen, was already a seasoned actress. Making her first stage appearance at the age of six, she had interspersed her schooling with numerous performances and, by 1939, was already destined for an international career.

It would be another fifteen years before Lister, who left

for England in 1943, and Sid would work together again. This time the series was called *Hancock's Half Hour*.

To his surprise Sid was offered more work by the SABC. Experienced and enthusiastic actors for supporting roles in radio plays were always in demand. Sid's fee had risen to two guineas a programme.

William Godfrey was another Rep member recruited by the SABC. His abiding memory of Sid was of a man totally dedicated to acting. 'Whether it was for radio or the stage, and no matter how small, Sid would really get into the part,' says Godfrey. 'During the run of a Rep production you would seldom find him chatting in the dressing room. He would sit on one side thinking the part. Thinking all the time until it was time to go on.'

Offstage, and despite his predatory attitude towards women, Sid gave the impression of being a 'lonely character'. He attended few end-of-run parties. 'You had to drag him to some of the parties,' recalls Godfrey. 'Once he was there he certainly enjoyed himself, but he always waited to make sure you really wanted him. Sid needed to be wanted.'

Returning to the Carlton Hotel one afternoon early in 1939, Sid noticed a new and startlingly beautiful face behind the reception desk. Her name, he discovered, was Meg Sergei.

Their meeting sparked an intense and mutual physical attraction. Meg was slim and well educated and breathtakingly attractive. Sid was experienced and witty and charming. Their affair was passionate and public.

Meg was three months younger than her lover. She had recently arrived in Johannesburg, but was dismayed to find no work for professional entertainers. She felt cheated by her own husband's promises of developing her career as a dancer. In desperation Meg took a job as a receptionist at the Carlton Hotel. Her affair with Sid was enough to prompt Toots to file for divorce.

Thirty-five years later, during a drinking session with his agent, Sid is alleged to have admitted to Michael Sullivan:

'If it happened in the late 1930s I don't remember it.' It was a rare flash of honesty.

Hanna Opert, one of the Hearn girls and by now old enough to be included among his circle of friends, felt Sid had become 'killer naughty'. Between a series of affairs, a slow fatalistic slide toward near alcoholism, and several vicious and bloody fights, the only person Sid seemed intent on killing was himself. 'I am not saying he was an alcoholic,' adds Opert, 'but he would get good and high and that made Sid fight. When he was sober, which wasn't very often, he was a very nice man. But when he had had a few drinks all he wanted to do was fight.'

Popular legend has it that Sid acquired his battered face and mushy ears during a career as a semi-professional boxer. 'I used to fight as a middle-weight,' he told one interviewer in the sixties. 'The biggest purse I ever got was fifty-bob and it was in that fight I had my nose broken. The doc fixed it but it broke again. Then my ears were a bit puffy after another fight and I cried enough.'

In private Sid liked to amuse his future friends by claiming he had been forced to earn money fairground boxing. A story he once told fellow *Carry On* star Jack Douglas involved an all-comers challenge in a travelling booth. Sid would place a pound note under his foot. Anyone who could knock him off it could keep the money.

In reality Sid was nothing more than a bar-room brawler. 'Boxing? No,' refutes Opert. 'Boxing without gloves? Yes.'

One of Sid's 'girlfriends' was Sally Franks, his dancing partner from Kroonstad. Sally would often drink with Sid at one of the Carlton Hotel bars or accompany him to parties. 'He was a man I loved being with,' admits Franks. 'He was just a terrific guy. A lot of people were jealous of him and said he was a drunkard, but I know a lot of drunks who never get talked about the way he did.'

When he couldn't think of a good enough reason to hit someone Sid would needle a friend into starting a fight for him. One of the group's favourite haunts was Ciro's nightclub. Late in the evening a man approached Sid's party

and asked Hanna Opert to dance. Opert agreed. Her
boyfriend, a small, shy man 'who never hurt anyone in his
life', appeared quite happy to watch his date enjoying
herself. 'Are you going to let him get away with that?'
goaded Sid. 'Go and punch him.' To everyone's surprise
Opert's boyfriend marched across the dance floor and laid
the man flat. Sid waited a few seconds for the resulting fight
to warm up before wading in.

The boss's late arrival at Maison Renée with a black eye
or swollen face became almost a daily occurrence. Sid
refused to talk about the damage with his staff and joked the
bruises off with the customers. One injury was more
serious.

The political and social climate in South Africa had bred
into Sid a lifelong hatred of anti-semitic and anti-Jewish
behaviour. In many ways he was luckier than most. As a
second-generation emigrant, with a non-Jewish name and a
strong Cockney accent, he exhibited few outward signs of
his, by now, lapsed faith.

Joel Cohen, already a qualified surgeon, remembers the
growing pressures exerted on the country's ever-increasing
Jewish population. 'Anyone with a Jewish name had to work
twice as hard to prove themselves. If you were Jewish you
were suspect.' And it only got worse as the thirties
progressed.

South Africa was attempting to shake free of the
Depression by coming off the gold standard. And Jewish
refugees were pouring into South Africa through the ports
of Durban and Cape Town. By the late thirties the South
African Fusion government of Hertzog and Smuts was
under pressure to reverse the liberal and middle-of-the-
road policies of the past. It was under attack from both the
ultra-right wing and the extreme left. The Communists
were active among the 'natives' and encouraging them to
oppose entrenched white privilege. But the greatest danger
came from the right. Anti-semitism was permeating every
stratum of society as demands grew to curb the Jews fleeing
Nazi atrocities. Many people felt that despite its public

condemnations the government was taking too few practical steps to halt the wave of anti-semitic street violence. Attacks on Jewish premises in Johannesburg, Durban and Cape Town increased. Back-alley beatings were no longer commented upon.

At one party Sid was attending he overheard a blatant anti-Jewish remark. Sid tackled the man, not knowing that the big Afrikaner was accompanied by several equally well-built friends. The confrontation erupted into a near riot. Sid received a vicious beating; his nose was broken and both his hands were stamped on. One of his little fingers was so badly damaged it remained paralysed for the rest of his life.

Reine, who by now had expanded her boutique and was making corsets for her select clientèle, was shocked by her son's behaviour. They rarely spoke. News of Sid's exploits was also reaching other members of the Cohen family. 'At that time he wasn't charming or gentle,' recalls Joel Cohen. 'He was a real rough-tough type.' In many ways Sid was pre-living the characters he would later play on screen, 'and they weren't that different from reality'.

If they could keep up with his drinking, Sid's friends were not prepared to slug it out every other night – 'It just got too silly, too dangerous.'

Yet through it all, through the brawls and the beatings and the eternal hangovers, Sid never lost faith with his dedication to succeed as a performer. He still needed the financial security the salon provided, but his ambition to become an actor remained his one salvation.

With the Second World War under way Sid was persuaded, in 1940, to produce a fund-raising dance spectacular. The money would go to help refugee children. The only available location was the Jewish Guild Memorial Hall on Von Brandis Street. It wasn't the ideal venue; the hall had a small, sloping stage with poor lighting and only two dressing rooms, and seating was restricted to two hundred.

The show, Sid decided, would be called *Hoopla*. There was no shortage of volunteers. Among those who auditioned was a fifteen-year-old member of an amateur dance troupe by the name of Olga Lowe. Sid took the teenager aside and asked if she would partner him in a snowman number. Lowe readily agreed, but admitted that tap-dancing was not her strongest routine. Sid spent the next few weeks improving Lowe's tap technique.

That performance with Sid would remain with her for ever. 'We were tapping away when all of a sudden I looked down and Sid's willy had fallen out,' Lowe said. 'He must have forgotten to do up his flies. So I looked at it, screamed, ran off the stage and started crying.'

Still tapping, Sid danced his way to the wings, hauled Lowe back on stage and, out of the corner of his mouth, said: 'Come back here, you silly bitch. You'll see a lot worse than that before you're much older.'

As well as producing, directing and performing in *Hoopla*, Sid was also rehearsing for his first Johannesburg Repertory Players lead. It would be the company's eighty-first production. And Sid would give what many consider the performance of his life.

Sid had been invited to play the part of George in John Steinbeck's *Of Mice and Men*. 'From the moment he accepted you could see Sid was determined to make his character work, both for the play and his career,' admitted a fellow cast member. To fine tune his performance still further, Sid invited his employees from Maison Renée to the dress rehearsal. Many had never sat in a theatre before. At work the next day, Sid quizzed them one by one on his 'faults'.

Backstage at the Library Theatre on 5 April 1940, Sid sat in silence for almost an hour. 'No one had the nerve to approach him.' The curtain rose at 8.30 p.m.

'What I saw that night was one of the most extraordinary experiences of my life,' admits Harry Rabinowitz. Sid had given his character, George, a slightly strangulated voice and a hunched back. His friend Lennie – a great, hulking character – was played by Sydney Witkin. In one scene George breaks the news to Lennie that he is about to be

41

taken away. Sid turned his back on the audience and acted up stage, relying solely on his voice to carry the emotion. 'It was the most powerful piece of acting Johannesburg has witnessed in a long time,' was one critic's verdict. Most of the audience were in tears. Sid, too, left the stage sobbing.

Both women who had had brief affairs with Sid had been spirited away to Southern Rhodesia and were now living in properties purchased and maintained by the Delmont fortune. Despite the promises they had made to their newfound benefactor, both women in turn made secret contact with their former lover to inform him he was first the father of a girl and then a boy. Sid made no attempt to see or support his illegitimate offspring. To him they no longer existed.

Elizabeth James knew nothing of her step-brother and step-sister. She would discover their existence by accident more than two decades later. Elizabeth was growing up with no childhood memories of her father. He simply did not exist. She was seventeen years old when she met her father face to face for the first time since infancy, and then, she recalled, it was 'like meeting a long lost uncle – no emotion'. Elizabeth moved to Southern Rhodesia after her marriage to Benny Grevler in the 1950s. One day while shopping in a Bulawayo store she looked across the counter and was shocked to see herself looking back. 'It was like looking into a mirror,' she told friends. 'The assistant could have been my twin sister.' The most striking feature were the eyes. In his early years Sid's eyes were peridot green. Elizabeth – as all of Sid's children – had inherited the same yellowish-green irises. The women began to talk and, as their confidence grew, it became apparent that they shared the same father.

Once the divorce was final, Delmont demanded the return of Maison Renée. Sid refused, claiming it was legally his. The threats and counter-threats rumbled on for weeks. Delmont considered Sid's stubbornness a challenge to his authority and, more importantly, an impeachment of his

42

reputation as a hard-nosed businessman. There were several face-to-face confrontations between Sid and men sent by Delmont to retrieve the Carlton Hotel salon; on one occasion members of Sid's staff had to come to his rescue.

Early in the summer of 1940 Delmont was informed of the latest gossip circulating about Sid. Not only had Sid continued to flaunt his affair with Meg Sergei – a relationship which had ended his marriage with Toots – he was now having another highly passionate affair with one of his trainee hairdressers. More importantly, the seventeen-year-old girl (ten years younger than Sid) was pregnant.

In the late 1960s Zoe – not her real name – joined her son in England. She brought with her a faded snapshot of the hairdressing salon in which she had once worked. Standing with his hand on a young woman's shoulder is Sid James.

Her son, who has lived in England since his arrival in 1963, has inherited his father's crinkly hair and lined forehead. Like all of Sid's children he has suffered from a poor complexion. It was not until after the actor's death in 1976 that Zoe finally confessed to her son his father's identity. 'She never remarried and kept the secret all that time,' he said. 'But it was obvious from what she told me that she never stopped loving him.'

The ability to keep faith with that love, sometimes for decades, and despite the cruellest of treatment, is a quality shared by the majority of the women involved with Sid James. From Sid's point of view, the single-minded pursuit and seduction of an attractive young woman, while already committed to a relationship or marriage, was a life plan. Sid showed a consistent preference for big-breasted, slim-waisted women who wore their hair blonde, and Zoe – a 'well-developed, bubbly teenager' – was a natural target for his roving eye. 'Sid James took Zoe on as a trainee,' her son explains, 'and worked with her for a year without showing the slightest interest. Then, quite suddenly, he started to become very attentive and possessive – over possessive.'

Sid would make sure Zoe was kept busy until all the other staff had left the salon. It soon became apparent he had a different kind of lesson in mind for his youngest trainee. At first she was flattered by Sid's all-too-obvious advances. 'My mother was a virgin,' Sid's son explains. 'When she finally gave in, one night in the salon, it was more because she thought Sid would then leave her alone than in any hope of something more.' However, engulfed by a passionate affair and the excitement of after-hours sex, it wasn't long before Zoe found herself falling in love with Sid. One night she announced she was pregnant. 'My mother assumed Sid would be as overjoyed as she was; instead he went wild with anger.' It was the same response Toots' announcement had triggered three years earlier. Once again Sid refused to accept any responsibility. 'In the end, after a lot of tears and pleading from my mother, Sid completely lost his temper and struck her quite badly.'

Zoe returned bruised and tearful to her downtown Johannesburg home. Bullied by her father, she broke down and admitted she was pregnant. When she refused to name her lover her father ordered her out of the house. This time there would be no discreet offer of help. She never returned to the Carlton Hotel salon and within days had moved to Cape Town. In February 1941, she gave birth to a boy.

Whispered comments on Sid's latest conquest were replaced by open speculation about the overnight disappearance of the salon's teenage trainee. This time Joe Delmont would not intervene, but something had to be done to curb the sexual appetite of his former son-in-law and ensure Sid's impregnation of a third hairdresser associated with the salon – a salon Delmont publicly claimed he owned – did not breathe life into old and highly damaging gossip. Sid, the old man decided, no longer needed to be taught a lesson – he needed to be punished.

Delmont promptly put a price on Sid's head. The nature of the 'contract' was less specific. One rumour that reached Sid claimed Joe Delmont wanted Sid 'removed' for good. Another more specific warning suggested it was only certain parts of Sid's anatomy that were to be removed – as painfully as possible.

Whatever the exact instructions the men hunting Sid had been given, he was taking no chances. He no longer went to work, only coming out of hiding to attend rehearsals for Oscar Wilde's *The Importance of Being Earnest*. On his way home one night he outwitted and outran his pursuers. The city was becoming too dangerous. After a final performance as an amateur actor, Sid James decided it would be safer being a professional soldier.

CHAPTER FOUR

General Jan Smuts had worked long and hard to turn his country's rag-bag army into an effective fighting force – he wasn't about to let it be overrun by a bunch of namby-pamby actors.

When South Africa declared war on Germany on 5 September 1939, the Union's permanent defence force had dwindled to a mere 1,350 men. It was ill-trained and ill-equipped; there were no spare uniforms and few rifles in store. The country's two home-made armoured cars were supplemented by a couple of tanks and a few guns, all veterans of the First World War. The navy consisted of one ship, HMSAS *Botha*, an engineless training ship moored at Simonstown.

Smuts, the supreme realist, admitted the men and women of his new armed forces needed moral as well as material support. Boredom in the military camps was one battle his officers could do without. When Major-General F. H. Theron, the Union Defence Force adjutant general, approached his superior with a plan to appoint an entertainment officer, Smuts conceded the logic of the idea. He demanded one condition: all uniformed entertainers should be soldiers first and performers second.

The embryonic unit, which so far existed solely on paper, was given the grandiose title of the No. 19 Reserve Transport Company. Now all Theron had to do was turn it into a fighting – and singing and dancing – unit.

The man he chose for the job was Major Myles Bourke, the founder of the Pretoria Repertory Theatre. As the UDF's only entertainment officer, Bourke submitted a report on the 'militarisation' of troop entertainment. The problem was immense. He estimated that to effectively tour all the Union bases and the war zones in North Africa he would require at least eighteen separate concert parties. So far he didn't even have a permanent office.

The wrangling began. Not only between Bourke and the military hierarchy, who saw his plans as overly ambitious, but between Bourke and other units loath to give up their existing entertainers. Eventually six members of the 'Springbok Frolics' were allowed to transfer to the new unit by their reluctant field artillery commanders.

Bourke was finally allocated an office at Defence Headquarters in Pretoria. As his second in command he appointed Frank Rogaly, an army captain with showbusiness experience. Hopeful applicants arrived at the office to be interviewed and auditioned. Among them was Private Sidney James.

On the first day of his basic training as an ordinary soldier, Sid submitted a written request to join Bourke's entertainment unit. On paper Sid's qualifications were excellent. In less than a week the posting was authorised and Sid was ordered to report to Bourke's cramped and noisy office in Pretoria. To his dismay Sid discovered he had swapped one kind of basic training for another – this time as a driver.

To fulfil Smuts' condition – and to justify its official title – every member of the Entertainment Unit needed to be a qualified motor mechanic or driver. Many, like Sid, had never driven before, let alone knew how to dismantle and service a combustion engine. In addition, the training course included specialist skills such as loading and transporting ammunition and driving an ambulance.

Many years later Sid was characteristically confusing over his army service. He claimed to have served with the Witwatersrand Rifles before his transfer to the Entertainment Unit. What remains of the regimental records make no mention of a Rifleman Sidney James. In other interviews Sid would hint at seeing action with the South African Tank Corps. Once again there are no records to support his claim. Equally confusingly, he once told BBC radio listeners: 'I joined an anti-tank regiment. I was in that for a couple of years, and then South Africa started up an entertainment unit.'

Possibly the truth lies merged within all three.

Throughout July 1940, the 1st, 2nd and 5th SA Infantry Brigades headed north from the Union to engage Italian forces in Abyssinia. With them went artillery, the Tank Corps, and motor transport units. It is feasible that Sid was training with one of these transport units while it was engaged in the East Africa Campaign. One thing is certain. Long before the fall of Mega – the Italians' southern Abyssinian headquarters – on 18 February 1941, Private Sidney James had been ordered to return to Pretoria and the Entertainment Unit.

To prove his unit's worth Bourke needed to produce a show as quickly as possible. While the major continued to lobby his superiors for a purpose-built home within the Pretoria headquarters, he transferred rehearsals to his private home nearby.

The scene which greeted Sid as he walked into the grassy residence resembled musical mayhem. There were dancing and choruses on the large veranda; ballet steps, leaps and jumps were being practised on the vast lawn; the sound of tap dancing was coming from two empty garages; from the vegetable garden came the strains of a violin playing Schubert's *Serenade*; on the hill at the back of the house the aloes and other prickly plants quivered to the sounds of Afrikaans liedjies and, drifting in and out of the chaos, was a dame comedian learning his naughty lines.

Bourke and Rogaly had dubbed their pioneer concert party 'The Amuseliers'. On Monday, 21 March 1941, they were ready to give their first performance at the Iscor Recreation Club, Pretoria. The audience included many of the officers who had scorned the unit's formation. Three months of intensive rehearsals paid off. A few weeks later Bourke was informed his unit would be moving from its single office to 15 Artillery Row, within the headquarters' compound. There rehearsal rooms, a small theatre, store-rooms and a carpenter's workshop would be constructed.

Bourke always looked upon the men and women serving in his unit as professional entertainers in uniform. As such, he argued, they should receive a comparable wage. His case was strengthened by the fact that members of Britain's Entertainments National Service Association – ENSA – all of whom were civilians, were living in houses or hotels while on tour and receiving as much as £10 a week. Bourke finally traded promotion for extra pay. All new recruits to the Entertainment Unit were immediately promoted to the rank of corporal. Performers were then up-graded to sergeants. By the end of 1943, when Sid was a staff sergeant, he was receiving three shillings and sixpence a day. Ironically, Sid would one day play the part of a weary ENSA comedian in the film *Desert Mice*.

In the final Johannesburg days before his enlistment, Sid and Meg had planned how they could spend the war together. Meg, far more than Sid, was distraught at the prospect of separation. As soon as Sid became a permanent member of the Entertainment Unit she volunteered. Meg Sergei arrived at Artillery Row just as the finishing touches were being put to the unit's cluster of huts.

Other pre-war friends were also finding their way to Pretoria. Muff Evans, who had known Sid as a hairdresser at the Carlton Hotel, joined the unit in October 1941. The musician Harry Rabinowitz arrived to work his way up to become one of the unit's musical directors. And in 1943 Olga Lowe, Sid's teenage *Hoopla* partner, joined soon after her eighteenth birthday.

Sid based his unit stage act on Max Miller. 'Based' is an understatement. His checkered, ill-fitting suit was an exact copy of Miller's, made for Sid by Meg. The patter, the pauses, the one-liners, Sid repeated parrot-fashion from the comic's records.

Miller's jokes were either very old or very blue. Ideal material for a male-dominated audience whose individuals spent most of their time wishing they were somewhere else.

49

Sid even filched Miller's catchphrase: 'It's the way I tell 'em, lady.' The audiences roared with approval. But Sid was learning – developing – something much more precious than mimicry. Miller had been blessed with the impeccable timing of a stand-up comic. Sid was replacing the measured pauses between Miller's jokes with a sideways glance or a shocked double-take. It was the embryo of a technique which twenty years later he would make his trade mark.

Before any of the concert parties were sent north they had to prove themselves by performing at the various military bases and training camps within South Africa. It was a valuable experience, both for the younger members and those, like Sid, not used to tight schedules and the chaos of touring.

One formality remained before the army would allow its entertainers out of their Nissen hut rehearsal rooms and into the 'real world'. Sitting in the front row of an otherwise empty concert room, the army's official censor was given a private performance. He weighed every word and nuance. The Entertainment Unit was never considered a security risk. The censor saw his job more as protecting the morals of 'innocent recruits'. Once a show's script had been passed by the censor it was a military offence to change a single word. The cheekiest of Sid's Max Miller jokes were the first to go, at least until Sid was safely in the desert.

Early in 1942 Sid's concert party arrived at the artillery school in Potchefstroom, north of the Vaal river. As well as his Max Miller routine Sid played Maingot in a selection of scenes from *French Without Tears*. After the performance he was approached by William Godfrey, his old Johannesburg Repertory friend with whom he had performed on radio. 'As usual he claimed he didn't have any money,' remembers Godfrey. Back in the unit's Potchefstroom hotel, Sid used a poker game to relieve Godfrey of some of his cash.

To the army, Corporal Sidney James was a member of the Union Defence Force Entertainment Unit No. 3. In company orders and on camp notice boards heralding its arrival in North Africa, they were known as the Crazy Gang.

The concert party included nine men and five women, among them Meg Sergei. By June 1942 the Gang was considered ready to commence the Entertainment Unit's 'Middle East Tour No. 1'.

Each concert party was a self-contained and self-reliant unit. Crammed into kitbags and large skips and old ammunition boxes were costumes, make-up, wigs, magic equipment, curtains, props, music and assorted stage gear. A portable stage was folded and packed separately. Instruments, the most treasured of items, were the responsibility of individual players.

Nobody was quite sure what lay ahead. From Pretoria the unit was transported to Durban on the east coast. Outside the port, U-boats regularly preyed on cargo vessels and naval convoys. The unit's personnel and equipment were loaded aboard a troop ship for the two-week voyage to Suez, followed by another cross-country ride, this time to a desert camp called Helwan, forty miles from Cairo. Here the Crazy Gang would help to establish a rehearsal room and northern base for future concert parties.

From Halwan the group toured the Western Desert, searching out units of the South African army. It gave performances among the rubble of shattered towns and in the open surrounded by sand and tents. Once the Crazy Gang was ordered to set up the stage in what appeared to be an uninhabited expanse of sand. As they prepared, and as if by magic, grubby and dazed soldiers emerged in twos and threes from foxholes and craters. They sat on the sand and watched the show. When it was over the rag-bag army evaporated back into the desert.

The days were long and the schedule exhausting. At the end of each performance the unit's lorries would bump and crawl their way anything up to two hundred miles to the next location. Nights were spent sleeping on the ground under bivvy sheets. If they were delayed by breakdown or enemy action the performers would dress on the way. 'You've never really put make-up on until you have done it in the dark in the desert in the back of a truck travelling at 50 m.p.h.,' Meg would say. If there was more time the stage would be erected; every costume was ironed and pressed and the empty three-ton trucks used as dressing rooms. Most shows were followed by an invitation to the sergeants' or officers' mess. 'You had to go,' recalls Muff Evans, 'no matter how tired you were. It was as much a part of entertaining the troops as the show.'

Back in Pretoria Myles Bourke was receiving news of his unit's first tour of the war zone – not from his performers, but from grateful officers. One appreciative colonel said his 2,000 men 'would never forget' the show. 'The Crazy Gang,' he informed Bourke, 'were the brightest and most polished' group of entertainers he had ever seen – in the army or out of it.

Sometimes the unit was forced to pitch and perform within sight of the enemy lines. In July, outside Tobruk, its convoy of trucks was first strafed and then bombed by the Luftwaffe. There were no serious injuries but most of the equipment was damaged. For days, and in what seemed to Sid almost a personal grudge, the German air force harried the concert party. More gear and costumes were lost. Major Bourke was informed the Gifts and Comforts Committee was 'trying to replace what was lost at Tobruk and after'.

The tour lasted eight months. When the fourteen members of the Crazy Gang arrived back at Artillery Row in February 1943, all the corporals – including Sid – were immediately promoted to staff sergeant.

After the adrenalin and dangers of North Africa, things in Pretoria were settling into a disciplined but enjoyable routine. In many ways – and for the first time in his life – Sid had found the family and stability he had been deprived of in his youth.

As NCOs, he and Meg were billeted separately. It did little to cramp Sid's sense of enjoyment. Gambling and drinking and women were as important as ever. Now approaching thirty, Sid was older and more mature than most other unit members. 'He was a mentor – a devil of a mentor,' recalls Muff Evans. 'He simply loved the girls.'

To Evans, Sid was a 'most unattractive man', but he possessed the 'most terrific sexual power'. Part of this sex appeal was Sid's physique. 'He was broad shouldered, slim hipped, and he moved well because he was a dancer. He just stood there, said something funny, and the girls – all the girls – would fall for him like crazy. Not that he ever led the girls on, he didn't need to.'

Olga Lowe, at eighteen, saw Sid as 'charismatic and a gentleman'. 'You could not help but notice him,' explains Lowe. 'Once he came into a room you simply had to focus on him. Sid didn't walk into a room – he arrived.'

Lowe arrived at a unit party wearing a bizarre hat. It had trimmings that hung down one side and over her shoulder. During the course of the evening a male guest became increasingly belligerent towards Lowe's hat. 'Being young and naïve I didn't want to say anything, but he was upsetting me.' Sid marched over to the man, informed him it was impolite to insult a woman, and threw him out.

'You were pleased to be in his company,' adds Lowe. 'He made you feel good. He was this big, butch, macho chap who treated women the way they wanted to be treated – like a woman.'

Meg, always the forgiver, watched and suffered. 'She had a hell of a time with Sid even before they were married,' adds Evans.

Meg's slim build and fragile, porcelain features were misleading. She was a hard worker who shared Sid's perfectionist streak. Meg could hold her own at a bar or around a poker table, and enjoyed proving it. 'There was always something to gamble on,' says Evans. 'Someone, somewhere, was running a book.'

Midday breaks were invariably spent at a bar off base. Rabinowitz, then a corporal, remembers: 'Sid and Meg would take me for drinks at lunchtime. That meant you left the headquarters at about twenty minutes to two, knocked back three double gins, and were back rehearsing at two o'clock. I could never keep up with that kind of drinking. Sid and Meg were in a class of their own.'

The invitation never extended to free drinks. 'I don't remember Sid ever standing a round of drinks for a crowd of friends in a bar,' adds Rabinowitz. 'I don't remember Sid expressing hospitality by spending money, not in the army nor after the war. It seemed he was always doing his professional thing, with the greatest bonhomie in the world – but the bonhomie did not spread to buying lunches or saying this round is on me.'

Sid's determination and professionalism were qualities Rabinowitz admired, particularly in an army, like any other, which survived on red tape and regulations. 'Sid shone as a leader,' he explains. Rabinowitz was not the only one who noted Sid's potential. There were now four separate concert parties either in rehearsal, gaining experience on the South African circuit or touring up north. As production officer, Captain Frank Rogaly needed an assistant. Sid had proved his ability to improvise after the Tobruk air raids. His stage background and pre-war experience made him a natural choice. Sid was commissioned as a second lieutenant and given the unofficial title of producer. Part of his new duties included auditioning new recruits. In a practical sense he was the unit's third in command.

Within days Sid applied to Bourke, as commanding officer, for permission to marry Meg and live off base. Both requests were granted. The flat they moved into was next door to Lionel Roche, the Entertainment Unit's wardrobe and property master, and his wife Meg.

Not long after his marriage Sid was admitted to hospital. He had been plagued with haemorrhoids since his late teens. This time his medical officer suggested an operation. When Sid was admitted to the army hospital at Robert's Heights he discovered the surgeon scheduled to operate on his piles was his cousin, Joel Cohen.

Cohen's examination disclosed the 'most horrible hae-morrhoids'. After the surgery it became a standing joke between Cohen and his cousin that Sid's piles stank of whisky. The operation was not a success and Sid went on suffering.

During one of their chats Cohen asked about Sid's parents. Sid admitted he had recently received a letter from his father for the first time in years. Lou, who by this time was in his mid-fifties, was in Australia. A few days later a cable arrived. 'Am in big trouble,' Lou pleaded, 'send £1,000.' In those days Sid was in big trouble himself, says Cohen. Sid replied: 'I'm pleased you haven't lost your sense of humour.'

It would be the last time Sid ever heard from his father.

By 1944 Sid was auditioning and accepting men and women direct from civilian life. All non-service volunteers had to be taught how to march the army way. The sight of comedians and ballet dancers and musicians flinging their arms in all directions and attempting to keep in step as they drilled up and down Artillery Row attracted an audience equal to any concert party.

One new service recruit was Joy Haines. A 'skinny, self-conscious twenty year old', she had transferred from the Women's Auxiliary Army Service.

Rehearsal gear for the unit's women dancers consisted of two pairs of long khaki pants with elasticated ankles and two pairs of large, black satin bloomers. Above the waist they had to wear white shirts or blouses. Sid, as dance director, took the first rehearsal of the latest women recruits to Artillery Row. Everyone had arrived in long pants. At the end of the sessions Sid reminded them it was summer and they should be wearing the black bloomers.

For the next five rehearsals, first two and then three and then four of the women arrived in the black-and-white outfits. Most had altered the bloomers to make them skin tight. By the sixth rehearsal Haines was the only dancer still wearing her khaki pants. Sid took her aside to ask why. Haines blushed and whispered in Sid's ear: 'Because my legs are too skinny.' In a mock-bluster Sid ordered the dancer to report to his office the following morning wearing the correct dress.

When Haines entered Sid's office she was still wearing the long pants. The bloomers – suitably altered – were

55

underneath. 'Right,' ordered Sid with a stern voice, 'drop your trousers.' Haines complied. After a few seconds Sid told her: 'There's nothing wrong with your legs and, from now, black bloomers, please.'

The matter was never mentioned again. But Haines noticed that Sid never selected her for a number which involved the dancers wearing the shortest skirts. Instead he gave Haines her own singing spot – accompanied by a backing trio wearing full-length evening gowns.

Early in 1945 the Entertainment Unit received one of its last recruits of the war. Within weeks Sid had threatened to 'punch his lights out'.

Larry Skikne arrived on Artillery Row fresh-faced and looking for stardom. He spoke with a broad American accent and told everyone he came from Cleveland, Ohio. Sid assigned him to the Bandoliers, Muff Evans' concert party. Evans was rehearsing a new show prior to her second trip up north. She soon discovered she had been landed with 'a very gauche young man'.

'He was so brash and he was so bad we wouldn't let him do anything,' explains Evans. 'We wouldn't even let him say a line on stage.' Skikne was relegated to carrying bags and dragging skips around. To justify his place in the Bandoliers, Evans kitted him out in a pink zoot-suit and revolting bow-tie and allowed him to sing a jitterbug number called 'Hey, Mabel, Wait for Me'.

Later that year, while touring in Italy, Evans found an ingenious use for Skikne's American accent and over-the-top acting. Whenever the Bandoliers were short of supplies, Skikne would don a US army uniform, arm himself with a shopping list, and brag his way round the local PX store.

Back in Pretoria Skikne's drawling accent was getting on Sid's nerves. Sid took Evans aside. 'For God's sake talk to that boy,' he told her. 'If he carries on with this phoney accent I'm going to clock him one.'

Evans yelled for Skikne. 'Sit down,' she ordered. Skikne parked himself on the stage like an obedient puppy. 'Look, we all know this accent of yours is pure crap. Stop it.'

'OK,' said Skikne, unfazed. The accent was gone. 'Anything else?'

Larushka Mischa Skikne was born in 1928 in Yonishkis, a Lithuanian town on the Baltic coast. His father, a successful and apparently far-sighted building contractor, increasingly feared the possibility of a Soviet invasion of his homeland. Papa Skikne decided it was time to start a new life in South Africa and, by 1934, the family had settled on a small farm not far from Johannesburg.

By April 1945 the Bandoliers had completed their tour of the South African bases and were about to leave for an extended duty in the Mediterranean. The night before Muff Evans' concert party left, Sid and Meg threw a farewell party. Peace in Europe was less than two weeks away. There was already talk of demobilisation and post-war careers. Little did Sid know that three years later he would help launch Skikne's career as an international star – renamed Laurence Harvey.

Sid strode down Rissik Street and into the old Standard Theatre. It was 14 August 1945 – VJ Day – and Sid was back in Johannesburg and looking for work.

In the repertory office at the back of the theatre he found the company's secretary, Irene Martincevic. A few minutes later in walked Muriel Alexander, the amateur group's founder. When Martincevic asked Sid what he intended to do now that the Second World War was finally over, he announced: 'Go to London.' Sid was still in his officer's uniform, recalls Martincevic, and 'ever so handsome'. Before he left, the trio had celebrated Sid's return with a bottle of champagne.

The war with Germany had ended three months earlier on 8 May. Other pre-war Rep members were beginning to drift back to the city. Within a month of his return from Stalag 18A, Harry Kahn agreed to produce the Johannesburg Repertory Players' adaptation of Paul Osborn's *A Bell for Adano*. Kahn had no hesitation in inviting Sid to play the lead.

Another of his recruits was Ian Kaminer, whom Kahn had asked to play Tomasino, the head fisherman, opposite Sid. During the first read-through of one poignant scene, Kaminer was shocked to see tears streaming down Sid's face. 'Dear God,' he said to himself. 'Such brilliant acting, what am I doing here?'

Adano – staged between 12 and 27 October 1945 – was to be Sid's last performance with the Rep. Technically, he was still a lieutenant in the South African Union Defence Force awaiting demobilisation. In reality, he regarded himself as an out-of-work actor. It didn't last long.

The war – which had syphoned off so many of Johannesburg's best amateur actors – also triggered the revival of its professional companies. The tremendous growth of the cinema during the 1920s and 30s had all but killed the professional theatre in South Africa. Overseas touring companies, those that bothered to include the Union, consisted of one or two well-known actors with a supporting cast of untalented unknowns. During the war years, a cadre of professional English and Afrikaner companies had established themselves. The foremost English-speaking company was owned and managed by Gwen Ffrangcon-Davies. She was among the audience at the Library Theatre for the first night of *A Bell for Adano*. Her company was about to depart for a tour of Rhodesia. At the end of the performance she went backstage to find Sid and offer him a job.

Unofficially, and quite illegally, Sid joined the company before his demob from the UDF came through. Sid's army pay was replaced by his and Meg's gratuity. The money soon ran out. Although adequate, the touring wages Ffrangcon-Davies paid Sid were hardly enough to support the couple's social lifestyle. Meg was keeping them afloat by dipping into a trust fund set up after the death of her parents in 1918.

In September, while the company was in Cape Town, Meg discovered she was pregnant. She waited until the tour was over and they had returned to Johannesburg before breaking the news to her husband. It was the wrong time to start a family, but at least Sid was acting. Meg feared Sid might once again see the arrival of a baby as a threat to his career. To her surprise he appeared genuinely pleased. His main concern now was how to earn enough money to support his growing family.

Extra money was available, but only if Sid and Meg left South Africa – a plan Sid had talked about for years. As an ex-serviceman, Larry Skikne had already received a government grant to help him travel to London and enrol at the Royal Academy of Dramatic Art. Other members of the Entertainment Unit were also 'training' in Europe. Sid and Meg applied for and received a £450 grant, enough to pay for their passage and tide them over until Sid could earn enough 'studying' acting in England.

There was another, more sinister, reason why Sid was eager to flee South Africa. For the second time in five years Sid found himself on the run. This time it was not a vengeful father-in-law but the infatuation of a former lover that threatened not only his career but also his marriage.

Within days of her company's arrival in Cape Town, Gwen Ffrangcon-Davies agreed to hire a young English actress whose own tour had collapsed, leaving her stranded in the province. Eileen Gibson was a confident and vivacious London-born actress who insisted on being called 'Gay' and used her long blonde hair and Cockney accent to ensnare any man she fancied. Watching a rehearsal on her first day with the company, there was only one man who gave off the kind of animal magnetism the twenty year old relished – Sid James.

For the first time Sid was the sexual prey, seduced by a woman considerably younger than himself, yet with equal hedonistic experience. The couple plunged into a frantic and dangerous affair. Whenever they were alone they made love – the opportunities made even greater by the fact that Gibson appeared to possess a contraceptive for every pocket she owned.

Back in Johannesburg – and by now aware of his

impending fatherhood – Sid attempted to disentangle himself. His lover had other ideas. Pleas and sexual promises quickly turned to tantrums and threats to tell his wife about the affair. During the second week in December 1946, Sid and Meg boarded the Durban train and a waiting liner for England. It would not be the last time Sid would hear of Eileen Isabella Ronnie Gibson.

Part Two

'I don't like this star business. I think, taking a long-term view, I am only a character actor, and I think once you start this star business you have got to wait for star parts to come along . . . and I don't consider myself a star.'

CHAPTER FIVE

Sid and Meg arrived in England on Christmas Day 1946. 'All I had was a burning ambition to make money,' Sid admitted.

The voyage from South Africa was rough and uncomfortable. Meg, by now five months pregnant, was irritable and scratchy. Even the prospect of returning to London after ten years failed to lift her spirits. When Mr and Mrs Sidney James stepped down the gangway at Southampton docks her mood was as chilly as the weather.

The couple had arranged to stay at 3 Queen's Gate Mews, a cobbled street of converted stables wedged between London's Queen's Gate and Gloucester Road. The house, when they found it, was at the far end of the mews. Sid and Meg soon made friends with the elderly sculptor Sir Jacob Epstein who had lived in Queen's Gate Mews since his arrival from his native New York in 1929. After their first introduction the Jameses went to look at *Rima*, one of Epstein's works on display in Hyde Park. 'It wasn't my kind of art,' said Sid.

In addition to a letter of introduction to playwright Emlyn Williams, Gwen Ffrangcon-Davies had also supplied Sid with the names of two BBC producers. On Boxing Day 1946, less than twenty-four hours after his arrival in England, Sid wrote three letters. The first was to Williams, seeking an interview. The other two, almost identical in content, were to Martyne Webster and Peter Richmond at Broadcasting House.

Using a broad-nibbed fountain pen filled with blue ink, and with slightly right-slanting handwriting, Sid outlined his professional career. He specialised, he told the BBC men, in American and Cockney dialects. He was also capable of handling tough-guy parts and some comedy. Among his 'leads' for Ffrangcon-Davies were George Pepper in Noël Coward's *Red Peppers* and in Emlyn Williams's *Wind of Heaven*.

Both replies arrived at Queen's Gate Mews on 2 January. Martyne Webster regretted that all the series he was currently working on had been cast until the end of March. The letter from Richmond was more hopeful. It invited Sid to an interview at Rothwell House on Thursday 16 January, at 11.30 a.m. There is no record on the BBC files of what the meeting achieved.

There had been no letter from Emlyn Williams. It was now Sid's turn to feel frustrated. To cheer themselves up, Sid and Meg decided to take a walk through London's theatreland. Meg also wanted to show Sid her pre-war haunts. As they strolled down Shaftesbury Avenue Sid and Meg became aware of two familiar faces hurrying towards them. It was Olga Lowe and her actor husband, John Tore. Both had been members of the last Entertainment Unit party to tour the Mediterranean bases and had remained in Cairo after the war. Sid and Meg had not seen them since the spring of 1945.

'How the hell do you get started in this place?' asked Sid, once the greetings were over.

Lowe and Tore explained that they were on their way to an audition at their agent's office in Golden Square, Soho. They had arrived in England early in 1946 with a letter of introduction to the theatrical agency of Archie Parnell and Company. Since Parnell's death his widow, Phyllis Parnell, had taken over the business. It was a good time for anyone attempting to break into the British film industry. Equity had little more than 8,000 registered actors and actresses on its books and few experienced character actors. The film parts were small, but there were more than enough to go round.

Tore explained he and his wife had been asked to audition as a gangster and his moll. 'You look more like a gangster

64

than I do,' Tore suggested to Sid. 'Why don't you go up for the gangster's part and Olga can try for your moll?'

When they arrived at the Golden Square office, Phyllis Parnell agreed to the swap and introduced Sid to director Oswald Mitchell. The film he was casting was called *Black Memory*. Thirty minutes later Sid had been offered the role of Eddie Clinton. Lowe was rejected for the part of his moll. Sid felt obliged to let Parnell represent him. Nine days after his arrival in England Sid had landed both a film part and an agent.

The film's star was Michael Atkinson. As a boy he runs away from reform school after being tormented by a youth who had given evidence that sent Atkinson's father to the gallows. Years later he returns to extract a confession and clear his father's name. The film was a quickie – which most critics of the day unanimously described as 'miserable' – and only guaranteed a showing under the British Screen Quota Act. When *Black Memory* was released in Sid's native South Africa it was feared the title would put off white cinemagoers. It was subtly retitled *Dark Memory*.

While shooting *Black Memory* at Bushey, just outside London, Sid made friends with fellow actor Michael Medwin. 'Mickey liked my work,' explained Sid. 'He was friendly with a producer called Harold Huth, who was doing a film called *Night Beat*, and I walked straight into that part.'

Filmed in the late spring of 1947, *Night Beat* was not released until the following year. The plot was strikingly similar to that of *Black Memory*, involving murder and an ultimate confession. Sid's role was uncredited.

At last, a letter arrived from Emlyn Williams. Sid went to see the forty-six-year-old playwright. They had tea and chatted and talked about Gwen Ffrangcon-Davies. Towards the end of their meeting Williams promised to 'try very hard' to further Sid's acting career.

Sid and Meg's stay at Queen's Gate Mews was temporary. In the window of a Gloucester Road newsagents they spotted a card advertising a bedsit. The top-floor flat was in a house at 1 Canning Place, just two hundred yards from the mews. The room was cold and poky, but Sid considered the house had a charmed life. Opposite, where a row of houses once stood, was a pile of bomb-blasted rubble. Other houses in the street had been hit by shrapnel. Yet the walls and windows of 1 Canning Place appeared unmarked by six years of war.

That weekend, the Jameses' last at Queen's Gate Mews, it began to snow. By the time they were ready to move in early February, the streets of London were snow covered and treacherous. Sid and Meg found they had swapped a South African spring for the worst British winter in decades. While Sid was away filming or attending auditions Meg shivered out her pregnancy in the cold and draughty flat.

On 26 April a London County Council ambulance collected Meg from Canning Place and took her to the Royal Northern Hospital at Islington. That same day she gave birth to a girl. Six days later Sid called at Upper Holloway register office to record the arrival of his latest daughter. The baby was named Reine Christina James after both Sid and Meg's mothers.

It soon became obvious that the flat was no place to raise a baby. The room was cramped and awkward, and shopping and baby had to be dragged up three flights of stairs. Phyllis Parnell was shocked to see the conditions in which her latest client was living. Sid and Meg decided it was time, once again, to dip into the New Zealand trust fund.

Sid felt they deserved better. He needed an address in keeping with his ambitions and Parnell's promise that 'people were at last showing an interest'. In May they took a furnished apartment in Allan House, an impressive red-brick and white-stone block just round the corner from Kensington High Street. It was their first real home. Over the next three years it would become a meeting place for a growing band of South African expatriates and many of London's up and coming stars.

On 20 August Sid signed a standard BBC contract to

appear in the first six episodes of the Light Programme drama, *The Fabulous Miss Dangerfield*. The series would be produced by Cleland Finn, who gave Sid the part of Bill. Each episode would involve twelve-and-a-half hours' work, for which Sid was paid ten guineas. Rehearsals and recording were to be split between Broadcasting House and the Grafton Studio. The thirty-minute episodes were broadcast weekly from 4 September.

By December Sid had been offered a second radio part, this time in 'Interlude at Augusta', the second episode of *Paul Temple and the Sullivan Mystery*. He was paid eight guineas, one of the lowest fees he would ever receive from the British Broadcasting Corporation, and possibly the lowest in his entire thirty-year British career.

The year would also share another low – and high – water mark. Before the first anniversary of his arrival in Britain Sid had acted in five films. They would include the worst, and arguably one of the best, in which he was involved. His roles in both films were too small to warrant a credit.

Because of its reputation as a minor Ealing classic, *It Always Rains on Sunday* is frequently cited as Sid James's first British screen appearance. In fact he had already worked on *Black Memory* and *Night Beat* and had a walk-on part in the Eric Ambler story, *The October Man*.

Although he would only ever make five films for the Ealing Studio, all would play a major part in advancing Sid's career. *It Always Rains on Sunday* was directed by Robert Hammer. It tells the story, now rather dated, of an escaped convict's refuge in his married mistress's East End house. Among its stars were Jack Warner and Googie Withers. The *Sunday Times* film critic commented: 'Let me pay it the simplest of compliments and say it has the persuasiveness of an exciting story professionally told.'

Late in 1947 Phyllis Parnell was contacted by Oswald Mitchell to see if Sid would be interested in a small part in his latest film. Mitchell, as a director, had given Sid his first film part. Now he was co-producing an adaptation of James Hadley Chase's crime novel, *No Orchids for Miss Blandish*.

The plot concerns the kidnap of an American heiress who becomes increasingly infatuated with the gang's psychopathic leader. The book was a bestseller. When it was released the next year, the film was unanimously dubbed the 'worst film ever made'.

The *Daily Express* claimed the film's 'morals are about level with those of a scavenger dog'. Milton Schulman, writing in the London *Evening Standard*, described it as the 'most vicious display of sadism, brutality and suggestiveness' he had ever witnessed. The most decisive attack came from the trade publication, *MFB*. It reported: 'This must be the most sickening exhibition of brutality, perversion, sex and sadism ever to be shown on a cinema screen . . . with pseudo-American accents the actors literally battle their way through a script laden with suggestive dialogue.'

Early on Saturday, 25 October 1947, while Sid James and his wife and young daughter were still asleep in their Allan House apartment, a Union Castle liner was being nudged gently into its berth at Southampton docks. By nightfall Sid's name would be linked to one of the most notorious sex scandals and murders of the post-war years.

As the *Durban Castle*'s passengers enjoyed breakfast before disembarkation, one of the ship's crew was being discreetly spirited ashore handcuffed to a policeman. In the half-light of dawn James Camb was driven the mile to Southampton police headquarters, which adjoined the city council offices and was built from the same impressive white stone. Questioned by detectives, the thirty-year-old deck steward repeated the story he had told the ship's master-at-arms ten days earlier.

The day after the liner left Cape Town on its way to England the Glasgow-born steward struck up a conversation with a female passenger. The woman introduced herself as Gay Gibson. It was soon obvious to Camb, as well as several of the liner's male complement, that the attractive passenger expected – even demanded – far more than the usual ship-board service. Camb was certainly not going to turn down a whispered invitation to spend the night with a beautiful woman.

Gay Gibson opened the door of cabin 126 naked beneath a black silk dressing gown, and the pair wasted no time. Gibson was a wild and demanding lover, but beneath Camb the woman's body suddenly went strangely rigid. She was no longer breathing. Her eyes were fixed and staring; her lips were a greyish-blue. Panic gripped the steward. There was no pulse. Gibson, for whatever reason, had died in the throes of intercourse.

'I couldn't think clearly,' Camb told the police. 'I knew I had to get rid of her. The Union Castle liner was ninety miles off the coast of Portuguese Guinea, West Africa. Opening the cabin porthole he slid the actress's naked body into the darkness, tossing her dressing gown and pyjamas after it. Gibson's body was never found. Later that day James Camb gave himself up.

A second police car delivered the actress's trunk and case to Southampton police station. Officers began sifting the contents for further evidence. Near the bottom of the leather-bound trunk were two diaries and a bundle of personal papers. Reading through the scribbled entries – some graphically pornographic – it was obvious Gibson was returning to England to track down a jilted lover. It was now up to the police to find Sid James.

Southampton was still a relatively small city force and it was common for the chief constable to request the help of Scotland Yard with murders and other serious crimes. On 28 October – three days after the *Durban Castle*'s arrival he officially asked the Metropolitan Police to trace and question Sid James.

It was not a difficult task. Sid James's face had not yet gained instant recognition. His voice, however, which still carried a slight South African lilt, could be heard each week in *The Fabulous Miss Dangerfield*. The detective sergeant assigned to the case was a fan of the BBC serial and telephoned Broadcasting House to get the actor's address.

'When I rang Mr James at home,' recalls Rowland McArthur, 'he was very agitated and insisted his wife should not be informed. I found that a little odd considering I had not told him what our inquiries concerned.'

Sid arranged with McArthur, who died in 1996 after serving with the Hong Kong police as a detective chief inspector, to meet at his agent's Golden Square office. From what the detective sergeant learned from his Southampton colleagues it was obvious Sid had played no direct part in the death; James Camb had already been charged with murder and had appeared in court. 'There was a possibility – just a possibility at that stage – that Mr James had somehow arranged for her to be killed,' said McArthur. 'When I asked Mr James if he knew the name Eileen Isabella Ronnie Gibson he went deathly white and started to shake. I'll always remember him holding the edge of the desk trying to stop his hands from shaking.'

Sid decided to come clean. He admitted the affair and claimed Gibson was a 'nymphomaniac who refused to let go'. He was, explained Sid, the victim of the actress's obsessive passion and lurid imagination – a claim supported by the diaries and papers found in the dead woman's luggage.

McArthur found Sid a 'charming and plausible individual'. Had the detective sergeant known more of Sid's past – as a lecherous amoral womaniser with a history of violence – he would certainly have dug deeper. In Southampton Camb denied any connection with the actor, claiming never to have heard of Sid James. A week later McArthur interviewed Sid a second time, again at his agent's office, and informed the actor Scotland Yard's involvement in the case was over.

The following March, while Sid was enjoying his first West End success, James Camb was found guilty by a Hampshire Assizes jury at Winchester of the murder of Eileen Gibson. The court was told nothing of Sid James's connection with the victim. After a four-day trial Camb was sentenced to death. Within a month the Home Secretary granted him a reprieve.

Jack Hylton, the one-time bandleader turned impresario, was looking for new talent. He was a small man with a formidable reputation. Anyone Hylton put his faith in who failed to live up to his exacting standards soon found life increasingly uncomfortable. Those who pleased the Bolton-born businessman were rewarded with an unshakable friendship.

Sid arrived in Manchester to rehearse his part of a lovable drunk and drug addict in Hylton's new show, *Burlesque*. The part was relatively small but, as Sid readily admitted, 'the kind that got you noticed'. The show's stars were Bonar Colleano and Marjorie Reynolds. Colleano and Sid – the star and the bit-player – shared a sense of humour and an instant friendship. They would work together on two subsequent films, allegedly at Colleano's request.

Hylton's plan was to run *Burlesque* in Manchester through December and into January. If the show was a hit he would transfer it to His Majesty's Theatre in London. Sid took time off on Christmas Eve 1947 to telephone his mother Reine in Johannesburg. That same day Hylton informed the cast that *Burlesque* was indeed on its way to the capital. There was more good news for Sid. The impresario was so impressed with Sid's performance that the London production would include an extra scene written especially for the South African.

When Sid returned to Allan House that day, he found Meg spiteful and argumentative. Whispers of an affair had reached her. Sid had brought back with him a gaggle of new friends and – she was to discover – a wad of unpaid gambling debts. Off-course betting on horses and grey-hounds in Britain was still illegal. Bookies' runners, small inconspicuous men, inhabited most bars and street corners. Those who called to collect unpaid gambling debts were considerably larger and not averse to breaking a few bones. That evening Sid pleaded for time. To save her husband

71

from a serious beating, Meg paid off the debts from her trust fund.

Not all the callers at Allan House were unwelcome. The bejewelled and confident Phyllis Parnell had befriended Meg and was a regular visitor. Harry Rabinowitz, now also in London, was one of the guests at Reine's first birthday party. 'You didn't need an invitation,' Muff Evans remembers, 'you just turned up and were given a drink. Nobody minded.'

Another regular visitor, whenever he was in London, was fellow South African Rolf Lefebre. He had shared several leads with Sid in the Ffrangcon-Davies company and, not long after Sid's departure, had also decided to try his luck in England. Early in 1948 Lefebre was acting with the Old Vic company in Bristol. *King Lear* and *Treasure Island* were the kind of play Sid longed for – 'I always wanted my acting to be taken seriously.'

Even before *Burlesque* had ended its run at His Majesty's Theatre, Sid was offered a part in a West End production of the Jean-Paul Sartre play, *Men Without Shadows*. Also in the cast was Kathleen Byron. She would become another regular visitor at the Jameses' Allan Street flat, and was 'Aunt Kate' to baby Reine.

Other stage parts followed. There was a short run of satire plays at the Lyric, Hammersmith. Then the part of a singing hoodlum in *Kiss Me Kate*. In the autumn Sid would star in *Touch and Go*.

Sid's stage work had forced him to cut down on film offers. Uncredited walk-on parts, which took no more than a day to shoot, were accepted. Character roles had to be slotted between a musical or play. As Rowton in *Once a Jolly Swagman*, the story of an ambitious speedway star, Sid growls his lines as the hard-bitten team manager. And in the London Films production, *The Small Back Room*, Sid plays the part of an ex-boxer and barman called Knucksie who clashes nose-to-nose with a drunken wartime bomb disposal expert. To dress the studio set for *The Small Back Room* bar scenes, the director asked Sid to pose for a series of boxing

72

pictures. Sid stripped off and donned gloves, shorts and boxing boots. To complete the illusion, he was photographed in a specially constructed ring that included just half the canvas and only one corner.

Sid's British career was also gaining attention back in South Africa. In July 1948, the *Diamond News and South African Watchmaker and Jeweller* asked: 'Do you remember him?' The news item is worth reproducing as much for its inaccuracy – most of the details were supplied by Sid – as for his growing reputation.

> *Soon to be seen again in South Africa, but on the screen, is Sydney James* [sic]. *Born in South Africa in 1913 with his parents both on the stage, he made his first appearance on it at the age of ten.*
>
> *But later in a varied career, he spent some years in the diamond industry. He started as an apprentice in the industry ending as a diamond polisher with the firm of D Pearson of Johannesburg, who are now out of business. With his brother Maurice he took part in the Grasfontein diamond rush, staking a claim. His other jobs include working as a dock hand in Durban and as a coal heaver. Yes, he's tough.*
>
> *After the last war he took up the stage again full time appearing in Johannesburg and touring Rhodesia in such parts as Major Joppolo in* Bel for Adano *and playing opposite Gwen Ffrangcon-Davies in* Of Mice and Men.
>
> *Mr James arrived in England 18 months ago with his wife and year-old daughter, Reina* [sic]. *Within a week he had a stage part. They were followed by many others. Now he is making his first film, playing the part of an ex-pugilist bar-tender in the Nigel Balchin story* The Small Back Room. *The first part should be easy for he is an amateur boxer, and his film bar includes some of his fight photographs.*

Margaret Kidman, with whom Meg had shared a flat in pre-war London, was staying at Allan House. 'Sid was lively and

73

talented and almost always working,' she recalled. 'But it was Meg who had the money.' Two or three times a week during the run of *Kiss Me Kate*, Meg and Kidman would meet Sid at the theatre after the performance. The trio would then go for a late meal or spend the early hours dancing at the 21 Club, or the Coconut Grove, or Chandalls. Other actors and actresses would join the party. Adds Kidman: 'Sid was invariably drunk but he was always good fun.'

Several of Sid's South African friends travelled to London after the war. After watching *Kiss Me Kate*, one former employee of the Carlton Hotel salon called at the stage door to see Sid, where it was suggested they go for a drink. 'I'm sorry,' Sid apologised, 'but I'm broke. Can you lend me a few quid?' After a couple of drinks Sid made his excuses and left. The money was never repaid. It was a ploy Sid would use on his long-lost friends on more than one occasion.

On 1 September 1939 – during a Mickey Mouse cartoon – the screens of the 5,000 or so television sets receiving BBC programmes in the London area suddenly went blank. The Government feared the transmissions from the Alexandra Palace mast could be used as a homing device by German bombers. Seven years later, on 7 June 1946, the same Walt Disney cartoon reopened the service. Announcer Leslie Mitchell quipped: 'As I was saying before we were so rudely interrupted . . .' And Jasmine Bligh asked: 'Hello, do you remember me?'

Sales of television sets were booming, although it wasn't until 1949 that viewers in the Midlands were first able to watch BBC programmes. So far television was seen as a London entertainment and a threat to the capital's traditional venues. Most variety agents blacklisted any artist who appeared on television. The Stoll Theatre banned Ivy Benson and her all-girl band from a BBC television booking. Phyllis Parnell had no such qualms.

It was in a studio at Alexandra Palace that Sid achieved

his first lead since landing in England twenty months earlier. His introduction to the new medium was both rapid and hectic. On 1 and 5 August 1948, Sid played Sharkey Morrison in both episodes of *Kid Flannagan*. Ten days later TV audiences saw him again, this time playing the lead of Billy Johnson in another two-part drama, *The Front Page*. For both productions he netted a total of ninety-five guineas.

By some quirk of fate, not unnoticed by Sid, his career would be dogged by a series of 'double-takes'. A role he was playing, or even the setting of a film, would be followed by something very similar. Only days after Sid's TV appearance in *The Front Page*, he was filming *Paper Orchid*, an unsuccessful attempt to combine love and murder with the excitement of Fleet Street. The film – in which Sid played the drunken young crime reporter Freddie Evans – starred Hugh Williams and Hy Hazell.

The nineteen-year-old actress was nervous enough without being pestered by Sid James. At first she had been flattered by his obvious attention. A brief smile at rehearsal; a nod as they passed in the corridor. And then the invitations to dinner. For three months, Valerie Ashton had turned him down. Now he was beginning to irritate her. He was 'conceited and arrogant', and there was no way she would go out with a married man fifteen years her senior.

Valerie Elizabeth Patsy Assan was born on 13 December 1928, at the family's West Hartlepool home. As soon as she was old enough to turn professional, she changed her surname to Ashton.

Valerie had joined the cast of *Touch and Go* as understudy to Carol Lynne. She was about to get her big chance. Spotting how nervous the teenager was becoming at the prospect of taking over the lead from the flu-struck star, Sid stepped in with words of encouragement. Between his own performance and costume changes Sid watched from the wings. When the show was over he was the first to congratulate Valerie, and invited her out to a celebration dinner.

To his surprise Valerie said yes. 'In fact I only finally and very reluctantly agreed to have a date with him to shut him up,' she admitted years later.

That night, instead of returning home to Meg and his eighteen-month-old daughter, Sid took the wary Valerie to a restaurant. 'But what a difference when we were alone and away from the theatre and talking together,' she recalls. 'The great Sid charm hit me right between the eyes and by the end of the evening I was happily agreeing to see him again.'

In fact Sid's pursuit of Valerie Ashton was a classic James manoeuvre. Sid had supreme confidence in his own 'charm' and ability to talk any woman round. It allowed him to brush aside any initial resistance. The thrill of the chase was as intoxicating as the prospect of sex with another beautiful woman. Sid had employed the same tactic to seduce both Toots Delmont and Meg Sergei. It never failed. 'By the end of a fortnight I knew I was head over heels in love with him,' said Valerie.

Things were not good at Allan House. Despite the promises of a new life in a new country, it soon became obvious to Meg that her husband had not changed. Always a heavy social drinker, Meg began to consume more and more alcohol. When Sid arrived home, frequently with friends, Meg was very often drunk and almost always fractious.

Sid sought refuge from the constant bickering by spending still more time with Valerie. What started as an occasional day without returning to Allan House stretched to a weekend and then a week. Equally stretched were Sid's finances. By the following year he was effectively contributing – with what little money was left after his gambling – to two households. What irked Sid still further was the fact that Meg's trust fund was large enough to support both her and the baby without any contribution from himself. Sid appeared to ignore the fact that, for two years, it was Meg's dead parents' money that had effectively financed his gambling.

'Meg was convinced Sid would never leave her,' said a friend of the family. 'To Meg it was just another affair, another of Sid's fancies. One day it would be over and he would come home. All Meg had to do was wait.' While she waited, Meg drank.

For Valerie there was never any doubt. 'I knew he was my man. I couldn't imagine falling in love that way with anyone else.' She was not so sure her parents would agree. In 1948 she and Sid travelled north. 'I was only nineteen and terrified of taking him home to meet my parents,' recalls Valerie. 'I knew they'd disapprove, because of the age difference as much as anything else. But as soon as they met him they, too, fell under his spell and they really loved him.'

What Sid found was a couple who shared his belief in hard work, yet had the foresight to support a daughter who desperately wanted to become a successful actress.

By early 1949, 'silent' filmed sequences were often incorporated into television dramas, either as a background for titles or as linking material between the live studio scenes. One such programme was *Family Affairs*. Sid's agent had negotiated an eighteen-guinea fee for the thirty-minute programme – on condition that Sid provided his own costume.

Sid was appearing in *High Button Shoes*. Like *Burlesque* the year before, the show would preview in Manchester before moving to London. Awaiting Sid's arrival at the Manchester Opera House was a letter from BBC producer Michael Mills. After confirming the date and place of the filming, Mills told Sid: 'You are playing the part of an American film director and I suggest costume on the following lines – snap-brim soft hat, loud painted American tie, golf jacket/wind breaker, or similar.'

After completing his final Entertainment Unit tour of the Middle East and Italy, Larry Skikne had requested his eventual demobilisation direct from Cairo. He arrived in England early in 1946 and, after several auditions, was accepted by RADA in April that year. 'I was determined not to let my poverty show like some frayed cuff,' he later said. 'I never belonged to that school that believed scruffiness was next to stardom.' Skikne dyed his old army uniform black to wear to classes. Within a matter of months he was spotted by the director Jimmy Woolf, seduced, and as a reward given his first film part. Using the acting ability he had imbibed at RADA – and the cheek he'd employed in the American PXs – Skikne persuaded various Savile Row establishments to make him a blue worsted suit, a white silk shirt and a pair of handmade black calf shoes – all on credit.

Wearing his 'star's outfit' – and a borrowed overcoat to keep out the cold – Skikne had knocked on the door of 3 Queen's Gate Mews to welcome the Jameses to London and invite them to tea. Skikne was living in a flat behind Africa House.

When Sid and Meg arrived they found the entire apartment draped in red and gold velvet and sparkling with gilt trimmings. His flatmate was a flouncy fellow RADA student.

Sid tolerated Skikne, nothing more. At times, when Larry would arrive at Allan House arm-in-arm with a male and female partner, Sid found it hard to control his temper. Skikne's daring was all too frequently mistaken for arrogance. 'Humility is so bourgeois,' he said not long before his death in 1973. 'One must avoid it at all costs.'

But it was the Soviet Union which posed the biggest threat to his career as an actor. Despite having served in both the South African navy and army Skikne was still a Soviet citizen – and the USSR wanted him back. Lithuania's twenty-two years of independence came to an end in 1940 when Stalin incorporated the Baltic state into the USSR. Anyone who entered the war with a Lithuanian birth certificate now had it replaced with Soviet documents.

The Home Office classified Skikne as an 'alien' and ordered him to leave.

In a moment of despair Skikne decided there was no way out. He returned to the Chelsea houseboat on which he was now living, placed a cushion in the bottom of the oven and made himself comfortable. As he was about to turn on the gas he noticed the walls of the oven were caked black with burned fat and food. By the time he had scrubbed the inside of the oven clean he had gone off the idea of suicide and made himself a macaroni cheese instead.

There was one other solution. Skikne could remain in Britain if he could prove South African citizenship. For this he would have to give up his place at RADA and apply in person in Johannesburg.

In May 1949 Sid was about to open as Papa Longstreet in *High Button Shoes*. The London rehearsals were almost complete but Sid promised to have a word with the director on Skikne's behalf. A few days later Sid and Skikne were sitting on the top deck of a red London bus on their way to the Hippodrome theatre.

The discussion turned inevitably to Skikne's surname. 'You've got to change it,' Sid advised. 'It's not a name you can easily remember.' As the bus crept through the traffic the pair searched the streets for an alternative.

'Laurence Oxford [Street]?'

'Laurence Freeman?'

'Laurence Hardy?'

'Laurence Willis?'

'Laurence Woolworth?'

The bus pulled into a stop opposite the Harvey Nicholls store. 'OK,' said Sid, 'it's either Laurence Harvey or Laurence Nicholls.'

When the musical opened the following month Sid had persuaded the director to add the unknown Laurence Harvey to the cast. Reviewing the West End production, the *Johannesburg Sunday Times* claimed Sid has gained 'something of a reputation of an English Humphrey Bogart' for his portrayal of numerous tough, drawling heavies.

The similarity with Bogart had also been spotted by American studios. By the end of June producers at Plantagenet Films had offered Sid a part in the Brooklyn drama, *Give Us This Day*. Based on the story *Christ in Concrete*, it was renamed *Salt to the Devil* for US cinemas. This time Sid appeared ninth in the list of thirteen credits.

His third film that year – a spin-off from a BBC radio series by John Dickson Carr – would give Sid his first joint-lead. *The Man in Black* was an early Hammer chiller. By using yoga, a rich man (Sidney James) pretends to be dead, in order to expose the villainy of his second wife (Betty Ann Davies), who is trying to drive his heiress daughter out of her mind.

Sid was spending more and more nights away from Allan House. As friends on both sides remember it, the marriage breakdown was certainly not clear-cut. To Margaret Kidman the guilt was Sid's. 'A lot of the money went with Sid's compulsive gambling,' she says. Others claim that gambling had always been a part of their marriage, and that it was Meg's slide into alcoholism which prolonged, and eventually perpetuated, the affair with Valerie.

Reine James, who has no clear-cut memories of her early childhood, provides the most rational view of a complex and confusing relationship. She attempts to understand her parents. 'If you combine the fact that they are both people who'd had the most debilitating childhoods imaginable: neither of them had had security, nor been loved in the traditional sense; neither of them had been mothered; they were both insecure people; they were people who were constantly acting out their problems instead of trying to resolve them – so that, early on, he became a gambler and she became a drinker.

'And if you put two people like that together, who have just emigrated, who have got a baby daughter, so that he wants to go out, and feels guilty, or he is working, she is feeling trapped, he is gambling, money is a problem, she is drinking – what more do you want?'

It was, admits Reine James, a 'combustible partnership'

between two very immature people. 'I don't think they ever really understood how to be happy.'

The end for Sid and Meg's seven-year marriage came in 1950, just days after Reine's third birthday party. Sid turned his back on the relative luxury of the Allan House apartment and joined Valerie in a £5-a-week, one-room flat.

CHAPTER SIX

Sid turned off the road and stopped his car in front of the seven-foot-high metal gate. Across the top in white letters were the words 'Ealing Studios Ltd' and below, studded with reflective glass, the command 'One Way Traffic Only'. It was a lucky omen. A uniformed and white-gloved commissionaire appeared and swung back the gate. As Sid passed, the man stood to attention and saluted.

The stages at Ealing were situated in a two-storey building at the end of a long drive and at the rear of the production offices. Opened in 1931, it was the first studio in Britain to be constructed specifically for sound. Sid had worked there, briefly, once before. In 1947 Phyllis Parnell had driven him to the studio for a day's shooting on *It Always Rains on Sunday*. This time it was to have a more lasting effect on his career.

Throughout the late 1940s and 50s British cinemas ran two feature films each week. The programme changed on Sundays and Wednesdays. Sandwiched between the Pearl and Dean adverts and the Pathé newsreel was a low-budget, low-quality film the industry euphemistically described as a B-movie. Early in 1951 Phyllis Parnell was approached by director Charles Crichton. He had seen a rugged, gravel-throated actor in a B-movie – Crichton could never recall exactly which – and believed the man was on Parnell's client list. It soon became apparent that the man he wanted was Sid James.

Crichton was about to shoot a new comedy for the Ealing Studio. It had been written by T. E. B. Clarke, who would win an Academy Award for his script, and centred around a plan to smuggle gold to the Continent. Crichton had already secured the services of Alec Guinness and Stanley Holloway; what he wanted now was someone to play the Cockney safe-cracker Lackery. The film, Crichton mentioned, was called *The Lavender Hill Mob*. It would be the first time Sid had been engaged for a film conceived and produced for distribution as a main feature.

During his days off, or occasionally at weekends, Sid would return to Allan House to see Meg and play with his daughter. The separation had defused the tension. The visits would be friendly and full of laughter. Sometimes Sid would take Reine for a walk in nearby Holland Park or all three would go shopping or have tea in one of the big Kensington stores. Meg would invariably pay. Reine's earliest memory of her father is of one of these visits. She is performing a song and dance number from *High Button Shoes*. Sid is watching from an armchair. When his daughter finishes she bows and Sid claps and cuddles her.

Another regular caller at Allan House was Muff Evans. She was now working in England as a beautician and make-up specialist. Many years later, when Reine was a teenager, the telephone rang in Evans' London flat. It was Reine. 'Auntie Muff . . .' The voice was trembling. 'Will you tell me the truth? Did my father really love me?'

Evans shared a conviction with several of Sid's and Meg's friends that Sid was finding it hard to let go. Yet through the bravado of the break-up Sid still worried about his daughter.

Sid was always conscious of his skin problems. During the final weeks of his marriage – and when the prospect of unemployment loomed – his neck would erupt in a cluster of angry carbuncles. Giving Muff Evans a lift home one night from Allan House Sid asked: 'You know the problems I've had with my skin – do you think Reine will have that trouble?' Evans attempted to reassure him. 'Will you watch her for me?' he asked.

Other friends and colleagues were also recruited to watch over his daughter. Aunt Kate – Kathleen Byron – and Sid's agent, Auntie Phyl, were frequently questioned on Reine's progress. 'He took you aside to ask you how Reine was, as if he didn't want anyone else to know.'

During the late 1940s Olga Lowe and her husband John Tore decided to write and produce their own musical. It was called *Golden City*. Prior to rehearsals for its Adelphi Theatre opening the couple hired fellow Entertainment Unit ex-patriot Harry Rabinowitz to help with the score. When the musical ended Rabinowitz found work arranging and conducting the music for ice spectaculars. 'I worked on four shows, but I just couldn't get up enough steam to accept a fifth contract,' said Rabinowitz.

While walking in London one day the despondent Rabinowitz bumped into Sid. After attempting to explain his lack of enthusiasm the musician asked Sid what he was doing. 'I'm working for Jack Hylton,' Sid replied. 'I've got a very good relationship with him. I'll ring him this afternoon and tell him about you. Then you ring in turn. And we'll see what happens.' Within days Rabinowitz had been hired to conduct the orchestra in Hylton's new West End production of *Paint Your Wagon*. Three months later he was conducting a BBC orchestra.

Meanwhile, Valerie continued her stage career with Sid's blessing. Early in 1952 Sid made contact once again with Harry Rabinowitz – this time to act as Val's tutor. Sid and Val had moved to a new apartment in Roland House in Roland Gardens, just off the Brompton Road. Rabinowitz was hired by Sid to coach and improve Valerie's singing. Two or three times a week the musician would call at the Roland House flat and put his pupil through her paces. Eventually, as Rabinowitz recalls, the 'master' demanded a performance. 'Sid came in from a day's filming, quite bright and cheerful, and Val fixed him with her eyes and said, "Sit down and shut up and listen to this." And we performed and Sid was absolutely delighted.'

On 17 August 1952 – after a two–year separation – Sid's marriage to Meg finally ended. He immediately applied for a special licence. Four days later he and Valerie walked down the steps of London's Caxton Hall as man and wife.

The brief ceremony was witnessed by Valerie's parents, Albert and Emily Assan. Even in the presence of his new wife and closest friends Sid was careful to reshape his personal history. He assumed his father 'Laurence James' was still alive and gave his profession as 'actor'.

Brushing aside the delay the divorce had caused, Sid justified the two years he and Valerie had lived together by saying: 'We first proved to each other that our relationship was going to succeed.'

As one of his friends recalled, 'Valerie was stronger and more determined than any other woman in Sid's life – except his mother. You got the impression Sid had to obey – not in any sinister way, but because ultimately he knew it was good for him.'

Sid and Laurence Harvey's paths crossed once again during 1952, this time on the set of the Ealing slice-of-life drama, *I Believe in You*. The film starred Cecil Parker as a former colonial civil servant who comes across undreamed-of realities when he joins the probation service. Parker is shown the ropes by a seasoned and unshockable Celia Johnson. This time Sid swaps his Lavender Hill safe-cracker's garb for a police sergeant's uniform. Harvey makes a brief appearance – before his departure for jail – as a young tearaway who corrupts a seventeen-year-old Joan Collins. *I Believe in You* was the first of nine films released during 1952 in which Sid earned a credit line.

In the eight years since the end of the war, Ealing Studios had earned a reputation for cosy whimsicality and earthy comedy. In 1953 it decided to exploit the community solidarity evoked by the steam train with *The Titfield Thunderbolt*. Said to have been inspired by the story of the Tal-y-Llyn Railway, which passed into preservation at that time, the film's scenario is the road–versus–rail argument, which develops into an all-out fight. It was shot on location in Somerset. Sid, who played Hawkins the traction engine driver, thought it would be an excellent opportunity to show his six-year-old daughter, Reine, a little of the countryside. One memory Reine retains of the holiday was sitting on a riverbank with her father and Stanley Holloway, the film's star, fishing for eels.

A variety of film offers – and screen professions – quickly followed. In the Monarch production of *The Wedding of Lilli Marlene*, with Lisa Danielly and Hugh McDermot, Sid plays an impresario. In *Will Any Gentleman?* Sid was the owner of a music hall. And in *The Flannagan Boy* – released in the United States as *Bad Blonde* – he was cast as Sharky, a fight manager. Sid's next role was as a Scotland Yard detective in *Park Plaza 605*, again retitled for American audiences as *Norman Conquest*.

Impressed by Sid's portrayal of Sharky and his pugnacious looks, executives at the Ealing Studios offered him the part of Adams, the owner of a boxing arena, in *The Square Ring*. It was a part allegedly written just for Sid. His addiction to cigars is also said to have been the inspiration behind Adams's habit of never leaving his office without a Havana cigar in his mouth. The single cigar survives by never being lit, until the climax of the film when it is matched while Adams is distracted.

Early in April 1953, an overseas telegram arrived at Phyllis Parnell's Golden Square office. It was from Hollywood.

MGM, which had secured the film rights to the long-running British service stage comedy *Seagulls Over Sorrento*, needed to broaden its appeal. To Americanise the original Hugh Hastings script, the studio called in Frank Harvey and director Roy Boulting. The film would be retitled *Crest of a Wave*; the lead was offered to Gene Kelly. To justify the film's setting of a naval research station on a small Scottish island, MGM drafted in a supporting cast of British actors. The trans-Atlantic cable confirmed Sid's part as seaman Charlie Badger.

Some time during the early summer of 1953, Valerie discovered she was pregnant. Sid was forty years old and Valerie would celebrate her twenty-fifth birthday in December.

Reine James – 'A charming and elegant woman with impeccable taste.'

Above: Sollie Cohen aged four – 'A grand boy, full of fun and laughter and with a terrific sense of humour.'

Right: Sid James with fellow Johannesburg Repertory Company member Sydney Witkin in *Of Mice and Men*, 1940 – the next day Sid joined the army.

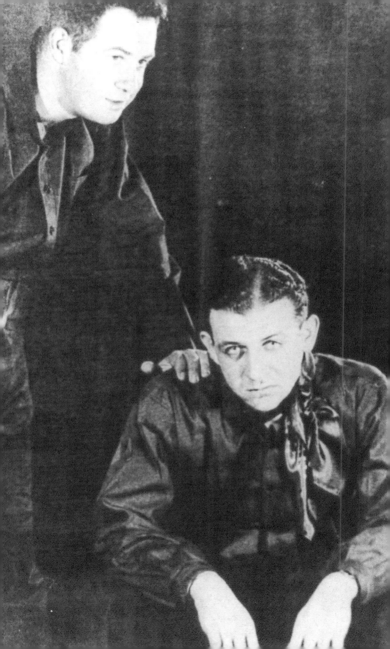

Above left: Meg Williams: she followed Sid into the South African Army entertainment unit to become his partner and then his second wife. They married in 1943.

Left: Sid and Meg performing Noel Coward's 'Red Peppers' number for troops in South Africa

Corporal Sidney James (far right) about to embark on a concert party tour of North Africa. Meg Williams is on the extreme left.

Rehearsals at the entertainment unit's Pretoria base. Lieutenant Sidney James (centre right) is in charge of production. Larry Skikne (Laurence Harvey) is at the microphone on the right.

Right: Meg – by now Mrs James – made all their concert party costumes. Sid's Max Miller routine was a favourite with the troops.

Below: Carry on Hitler: Sid and army friend Jimmy Quinn make use of discarded German props in the Western Desert.

With Gwen Ffrangcon-Davies in Emlyn Williams' *Wind of Heaven*, 1946. She gave Sid a letter of introduction to the playwright.

With Rolf Lefebvre in another Gwen Ffrangcon-Davies production. Sid would act with him again in the 1949 film *Paper Orchid*.

Sid always boasted his battered features were the result of his boxing career. In reality he was nothing more than a bar-room brawler.

For several weeks Sid had been on the brink of an affair with an actress in her late twenties. They had worked together for only a few days before Sid began displaying the first signs of interest. 'I noticed, accidentally at first, that he would be looking at me whenever I turned round. Then he would always be there to open a door or light my cigarette,' she explained. The object of Sid's latest infatuation is now married and living in the United States. Understandably, she does not wish to be named.

'The first time I saw Val I thought she was beautiful — very elegant for her age. It never occurred to me that Sid could be married to such an attractive woman and still make a play for me,' she admits. 'I may have been naïve, but at that moment even I didn't realise what he was up to.' That same day, and with Valerie safely out of sight, Sid suggested a 'candlelit dinner'.

'He was sexy, and very masculine, and very attentive. I had just gone through a rather messy relationship and I could quite easily have said yes. I didn't. I suppose I thought, "Right, you bastard, you're just another man, I'll make you grovel." And he did.'

Through Sid's eyes the innocent flirting had become a serious chase. Anonymous flowers would arrive in the actress's dressing room. Word would get back that Sid had been praising her in 'all the right places and to all the right people'. There were daily invitations to dinner. It was a copycat seduction of Valerie's, six years earlier.

'And then, quite suddenly, it all stopped. There was no more nonsense. No more attention,' she says. 'Sid remained a gentleman, but he never mentioned the "affair" again.'

In September 1953, Sid and Valerie attended the London première of *Is Your Honeymoon Really Necessary?* In the film Sid makes full use of his ability to slide into and out of any accent a director requires. For the second time in a year he had been asked to play an American. This time he was a gum-chewing, roistering member of the United States Navy Air Force. The comedy's star was David Tomlinson.

It wasn't the only American Sid would portray that year.

Group Three had been set up as a production company in 1951. Funded with government grants through the National Film Finance Corporation, its prime objective was to make low-budget films using unknown and therefore inexpensive new talent.

Group Three had hired Sid for two films during 1952. In the first – *Miss Robin Hood* – the company demonstrated its ability to capitalise on future talent by teaming Sid with Margaret Rutherford, Richard (Mr Pastry) Hearne, Peter Jones, James Robertson Justice, Dora Bryan and Sid's old friend Michael Medwin. It was also the first film in which Sid's character was also called Sidney, a device used later to cash in on his star status. *Time Gentlemen Please*, also released in 1952, was a sub-Ealing comedy about a lazy tramp's threat to the reputation of a prize-winning English village.

The following year Group Three contacted Phyllis Parnell again, this time to ask if her client would be interested in returning to Beaconsfield Studios to make a third comedy – itself a skit on the film industry.

Orders Are Orders, made during the summer of 1953, was a remake of a breezy British farce first filmed twenty years earlier and originally called *Orders Is Orders*. Sid played Ed Waggermeyer, the barking, rasping American film director; Peter Sellers played Goffin, a bored and bloated steward serving the officers of the 1st Battalion, Royal Loyals, whose camp Waggermeyer occupies while making a science fiction film; Eric Sykes – also credited with additional dialogue – is an army bandsman, and Tony Hancock the despairing bandmaster, Lieutenant Cartload. Hancock's stage-fright reduced his role to a liverish caricature. He certainly took little notice of his fellow actors, pre-occupied as he was with his first film part.

Recalling the film, Sid admitted 'it was a bit of a stinker'. He also claimed that it was during the shooting of *Orders Are Orders* that he and Tony Hancock first 'worked closely together'. They did meet briefly, but it would be another year before Sid and Hancock became friends, and at least three more before *Hancock's Half Hour* moved to television and Sid would genuinely offer 'little bits of advice, about two shots and close ups'.

The drought was over. Sid's pugnacious conviction and Valerie's faith had seen them through.

In a rare interview after Sid's death, Valerie said they were frequently short of money – 'Sid was out of work so often'. The flush of films he was offered in the last years of his marriage dried up in 1950. Phyllis Parnell – who silently disapproved of the break-up – secured several walk-on parts but only two credited appearances: in *Last Holiday* and *The Lady Craved Excitement*. Both were comedies. Radio work also ran dry. The BBC employed Sid only twice during 1950. On 6 April Sid made a guest appearance in *Filmtime*. Parnell persuaded the BBC to pay him five guineas 'out of pocket expenses'. Three months later he received fifteen guineas for a *Saturday Night Theatre* production of 'They Knew What They Wanted'.

Of that period, Valerie told *Woman* magazine: 'We tried never to be separated. If I had a job, say in Leeds, and Sid was out of work, then he'd come with me. In those days I often played principal boy in pantomime and Sid would sit in my dressing room mending my fishnet tights.'

The number of producers and directors making contact with Phyllis Parnell about her client had steadily increased. In the autumn of 1953 she was receiving up to four film offers a month. Ever conscious of an agent's duty to help shape a client's career, Parnell thought some too small or insignificant to consider. Others simply clashed. Sid, desperately short of money, wanted to accept them all.

In all, Sid received ten film credits during 1953. Perhaps his best performance of the year was opposite Alec Guinness in the adaptation of the G. K. Chesterton story, *The Blue Cross*. The film's hero is Father Brown, a Catholic clergyman-detective who retrieves a priceless church cross from the master thief Flambeau. It was shot, with Alec Guinness in the title role, during November. When it was released the following year, one reviewer said: 'Father

Brown has wit, elegance, and kindly humour – all somewhat rare commodities in the 1954 cinema.'

Valerie was on stage in Blackpool and lonely. She was missing Sid and her London home. The couple had talked about what she would do when the baby arrived, but Sid made no demands. Val, for the first time in her life, was ready to admit there was something more important than her career – 'How could you have a successful marriage if you weren't together?'

If she was going to turn her back on her childhood dream, Val decided the break should be 'clean and complete'. She first told Sid, who was 'delighted', then her parents, who were 'disappointed'. Trying to justify her decision, she said: 'I would rather have a successful marriage than a successful career.'

By the end of January Sid had agreed to take over the male lead in Damon Runyon's musical comedy, *Guys and Dolls*. February was spent shuttling between rehearsals and their new home at 21 Lymington Road, Hampstead.

On Thursday, 19 February 1954 – just two days before Sid was due to start in *Guys and Dolls* – Valerie went into labour. Sid had long insisted his wife should have her first baby in the London Clinic, an expensive and exclusive Marylebone hospital. What Sid didn't know was how to get there.

Sid darted from room to room of the Lymington Road flat like a 'panicky hen'. After warning the hospital by telephone, he gently eased his wife into their dilapidated Ford Zephyr and headed across West London. As they approached Regent's Park, less than half a mile from the clinic, Sid realised he was lost. They drove round and round the park, with Sid getting 'more and more nervous', until he spotted a police car.

The two officers recognised him instantly. 'Don't worry, Sid,' they said. 'Calm down and follow us.'

Within a few minutes the patrol car had guided them through the traffic and pulled to a halt in front of the

Devonshire Place hospital. 'Sid was in a cold sweat and thoroughly exhausted,' Val remembers. 'I was far more worried about him than I was about myself and the baby.'

News of the birth – Sid and Val named their son Stephen – quickly reached the *Guys and Dolls* cast. When Sid arrived the following Saturday for his first performance he was greeted with a champagne reception.

First produced on Broadway in 1950, the show opened in London during 1953. The story is based on the 1930s writing of Damon Runyon, published under the collective title of *Guys and Dolls*. It centres on Sister Sarah Brown, who runs the Salvation Army Save-a-Soul mission in the Broadway district of New York. Her aim is to convert sinners to a life of wholesomeness and prayer. But the inhabitants of Broadway have other ideas, especially Nathan Detroit (played by Sid), who runs a floating crap game each night while attempting to avoid the attentions of his long-standing fiancée by day.

Among the audience during the early weeks of Sid's tenure was a twenty-year-old actress called Barbara Windsor and an ambitious young film editor named Gerald Thomas. For those in the audience who were to come to know Sid personally, his portrayal of Nathan Detroit was as close to the real Sid as any of his subsequent roles. 'Everything about the part, and the way he played it, was Sid,' *Carry On* director Gerald Thomas was to say years later. 'The part could have been written for him.'

Harry Rabinowitz agrees: 'When he became Nathan Detroit he came as close to his own character as it was possible to get.'

The similarity did not escape Sid. 'I loved the role,' he said. 'It was unquestionably the best role of my life – it *was* my life.'

Sometimes Sid would take his daughter, Reine, to the theatre to watch the show. The six year old would stand in the wings sharing peanut brittle with Vivian Blaine and watching her father dance and sing. Through a little girl's eyes it was magic and it was special and very important.

'That was when I got this very unrealistic fairyland feeling for the theatre,' explains Reine. 'It took me a very long time to see him as a whole person. I idealised him after that, and he was connected to that fairyland scene.'

But the distance which separated father and daughter across the stage would soon expand to fill a lifetime. Before the end of the year Sid would find a bigger and even more faithful audience. To Reine, the disembodied voice she recognised among the radio cast of *Hancock's Half Hour* would soon belong to a father she no longer possessed.

At a time when family life, no matter how disturbed or disruptive, should have been etched on to Reine's memory, she was forced to swap her private world for a public one, to share what, by a child's right, should be her own with millions of others. It appeared to Reine that not only had Sid deserted her mother, he had done it in the most public and hurtful way. As the years went on, and her father's reputation grew, people would praise Sid to Reine, unaware that Sid James was a stranger to his daughter. 'It was the most difficult thing to come to terms with,' she recalls. 'The man, as opposed to the image – and I feel cheated.'

It was a feeling shared during the summer of 1954 by another of Sid's daughters.

Elizabeth James was seventeen. She had just finished school. As a reward for completing her education, the Delmont family was paying for Elizabeth and a friend to visit Europe. After sailing north through the Suez Canal they would tour the continent by train, returning by ship from London. Toots, by now remarried, had written to Sid to announce his daughter's imminent arrival.

On the day she arrived Elizabeth telephoned her father's London home. Valerie answered. Her response to a woman asking for Sid James was 'very frosty'. It took Elizabeth several minutes before 'Valerie would accept who I was and pass the message to my father'.

Sid had not seen his daughter since she was three. When they met, Elizabeth burst into tears. Sid allowed no flicker of emotion. In the evenings, after his performance in *Guys and Dolls*, Sid collected Elizabeth from her hotel and took her to restaurants for dinner. Although he was occasionally recognised, Sid never introduced his daughter. He was also careful never to visit places frequented by his ever-growing circle of friends. 'It was as if I were a niece reunited with a long-lost uncle,' Elizabeth recalls. 'It was a wonderful holiday and he was very kind, but he was never anything more than an "uncle".'

After two weeks Elizabeth left London to return to South Africa. She never saw her father again.

On the first day of May 1953, a memo landed on the desk of the BBC's Head of Variety at Broadcasting House. It was an outline for a new kind of radio comedy. It would be played by comedians, but there would be no catch phrases or funny voices or long-running jokes. Neither would there be a musical interlude. It was a shift away from cosy, domestic-based comedy to a series following the misadventures of a central character and his associates. The authors of the outline were two young BBC scriptwriters, Ray Galton and Alan Simpson. The actor they had suggested for the thirty-minute show was Tony Hancock.

After several weeks of discussion the programme was given the go ahead. A provisional slot was found, more than a year away in November 1954. The task of developing the format was given to producer Dennis Main Wilson.

Tony Hancock had been spotted by Main Wilson while performing at the Nuffield Centre, a post-war London venue where ex-servicemen could get free entertainment. At that time Main Wilson was in charge of locating and auditioning new talent for the BBC. His first experience of producing Hancock came during the autumn of 1951. Hancock was playing a scoutmaster in an hour-long radio show called *Happy Go Lucky*. One of his 'scouts' was Australian Bill Kerr.

Four shows from the end of the run the programme's regular producer, Roy Speer, became ill and Main Wilson took over. He was not happy with either the format of the fortnightly show or its content. One of his first moves was to enlist writers Alan Simpson and Ray Galton. That October at the BBC's Paris Studio, an underground former cinema in Lower Regent Street, the pair first encountered Tony Hancock.

Within a year, Hancock had moved on to *Educating Archie*, a popular show starring a wooden dummy. By January 1952, research was reporting that many listeners considered Hancock the real star of the show. Hancock, still developing as a comedian, was already stealing the limelight from the long-established performers on whose programmes he was appearing. All four – Hancock, Main Wilson, Galton and Simpson – worked together once again on the 1953 series *Forces All-Star Bill*. BBC executives were debating the merits of giving Hancock his own show when Main Wilson was replaced by producer Alistair Scott-Johnson and *Forces All-Star Bill* by *Star Bill*. Meanwhile, work on developing the new show – still referred to on BBC memos and contracts as the 'Tony Hancock programme' – continued.

Galton and Simpson decided to locate Hancock's imaginary home in the dowdier end – the east end – of Cheam, a middle-class London dormitory suburb. The name had been suggested by Hancock himself. Throughout his life Hancock would be tickled by the sound of words. Whenever his agent Phyllis Rounce mentioned visiting her mother, who lived in Cheam, Hancock would collapse in a fit of giggles.

Within his shambling East Cheam residence Hancock would hold court. Galton and Simpson now needed a coterie of friends to play against Hancock's pomposity. First to be recruited was Bill Kerr. Not only had Hancock worked with Kerr on *Happy Go Lucky*, they also shared an agent in Phyllis Rounce. The embryonic Hancock would also need a forceful girlfriend, someone to 'take him in hand'. The ideal choice was Moira Lister. She was also working with Hancock on the final series of *Star Bill*.

To complete the trio, Galton and Simpson had a

character but no actor. Early in 1954 they had an actor – but no name. 'We had already decided we wanted a shady, crooked character,' explains Ray Galton. 'And we knew who we wanted for the part. What we did not know was his name.' The pair had seen the actor they wanted in the 1951 Ealing comedy, *The Lavender Hill Mob*. The film was now on its second release. Galton and Simpson tracked it down to a fleapit cinema in Putney. When they took their seats the film had already started. The man they wanted was playing Lackery. 'We knew that this wonderful face had always played crooks in films,' said Galton. 'But we had to sit through the entire film until the credits came up and we could find out his name.' The man they wanted was Sid James.

Dennis Main Wilson arranged a meeting at the Garrick Theatre between the rehearsal and evening recording of *Star Bill*. Sid arrived, unsure of what to expect. He was met by Galton and Simpson and taken to Hancock's dressing room behind the stage. The writers outlined the new series and, with Hancock's obvious approval, invited Sid to join the cast.

To their surprise, Sid appeared hesitant. The meeting was friendly enough, but Sid refused to commit himself. His main concern was money. Sid was less than two months into the *Guys and Dolls* run. He was also, he said, making around ten films a year. Just a few weeks earlier, in February, he had received just twenty guineas for an appearance in 'Another Part of the Forest', part of the BBC's highly acclaimed *20th Century Theatre*. Main Wilson could only offer five guineas more for each of the thirteen Hancock shows.

'I'm not really a radio actor,' Sid told Hancock, who assured him 'there's nothing to it . . . it's easy'. Sid ultimately agreed, with the proviso that if Hancock or Main Wilson felt the show was suffering because of his acting he would be allowed to drop out.

Recalling the meeting six years later, Sid claimed he agreed to do 'one show at a time . . . I really didn't want to do *Hancock's Half Hour*,' he admitted. 'At first I said no. I think I am a very bad radio actor. I like to work with my hands and my face, and I said, "No, I don't fancy it".' All three kept up the pressure. 'Then Dennis Main Wilson said, "Well, just try one." So I tried one, and then I tried two, and I'm very glad I did.'

The real reason for Sid's reluctance would not become apparent for another seven months. He was an experienced actor with a West End lead and almost fifty films under his belt. But he had never worked with a comedian before. What terrified Sid was the thought of being forced into ad-libbing. 'He was never a stand-up comic,' Gerald Thomas would explain years later. 'Sid would be hopeless without a script. Ask him to open a fête and he would be lost.' The prospect of Hancock galloping off on some flight of fancy terrified him.

Sid's BBC contract for *Hancock's Half Hour* did not arrive at Phyllis Parnell's office until the middle of October, just fifteen days before the first episode was due to be recorded. On the day Sid tried his best to smother his nerves.

The initial read-through went well. Late in the afternoon Main Wilson called a 'technical run-through' to check equipment and sound effects. He discovered Sid's hands were shaking so much he could not turn the pages without the rustle being picked up by the microphones. They tried placing the sheets of paper on music stands. This time Sid caused chaos by flourishing his hand and sending the stands crashing down and the pages fluttering across the stage.

Hancock went out first to warm up the audience. When he was joined by the rest of the cast, Sid shuffled on stage with his trilby pulled down over his eyes and the script hiding the rest of his face. 'He was shaking with fear,' remembers Alan Simpson. 'He was petrified of the audience.' The recording had to be stopped several times. Sid was holding the script so close to his face that all the microphone could pick up was a series of mumbles.

Moira Lister, who had not worked with Sid since the

SABC children's radio series in 1939, found him 'a lovely person, full of humour'. Of *Hancock's Half Hour* she recalls: 'At the time it was simply a job. They were terribly funny scripts and we enjoyed doing them, but it is only with hindsight one realised how brilliant they were.'

It soon became apparent, however, that Hancock was not an easy man to work with. 'From the start he was very neurotic and worried about everything. It was never a relaxed and happy show,' remembers Lister. 'Sid, on the other hand, was relaxed and easy-going. He was always on the ball and uncomplicated and knew exactly what he was doing.'

Lister watched the deepening friendship between Hancock and Sid more as a 'marriage of opposites' than two men sharing a professional sense of humour. 'Because Sid was un-neurotic, he was able to cope with Tony's neurosis and was probably a very good balance for him, both in the studio and out of it.'

It wasn't until the recording of the first *Hancock's Half Hour* that Sid realised the series had also reunited him with another of his South African cronies. The distinctive theme – in which Hancock is represented by a tuba – was written by Wally Stott, and the version used for the initial broadcasts was played by the Augmented BBC Revue Orchestra, conducted by Harry Rabinowitz.

Kenneth Williams joined the *Half Hour* team from the first programme. Main Wilson had recruited Williams after seeing him as the Dauphin in Shaw's *Saint John* at the Arts Theatre.

From the start there was an antipathy between Sid and Williams which, although it remained submerged throughout the next twenty-two years, was evident to anyone who knew both men. Although they worked well together – producing some of the funniest *Hancock's Half Hour* sketches and *Carry On* scenes – their backgrounds and personal self-image kept them fixedly apart. Williams's habit of flaunting his homosexuality was a problem for Sid – not so much for his sexual preference, more for his flouncy effeminacy. And Sid, who had effectively dropped out of school before his teens, found Williams's spiky intelligence unnerving. However, the biggest difference concerned their attitude toward acting.

Sid's philosophy for success centred on a tight, professional performance no matter what the style of a production or the type of medium. Williams, on the other hand, made a public spectacle of himself and chose to live as many of his waking hours as possible in front of his public – and he dedicated most of his theatrical life to making them laugh. His pointed nose and flaring nostrils were as immediately recognisable as Sid James's own furrowed forehead and tangerine-skinned nose. Yet Williams only needed the promise of an audience – any audience – for the fluting postures of his voice to go into overdrive.

A few years earlier, Sid had unwittingly let slip another clue to his future dislike of Williams. Harry Rabinowitz was at Pinewood to record a demonstration song when he bumped into Sid for the first time since the party to celebrate Reine's birth. 'You wouldn't believe what has happened to me,' explained Sid as the pair walked through the studio. 'People are clamouring for me to do their films because I know how to underplay a part. We are surrounded by people who overplay. But me, with my pock-marks and strange diction and funny smile, all I have to do is underplay a part and the directors love it.'

Hancock's Half Hour went out for the first time on the Light Programme between 9.30 and 10.00 p.m. on 2 November 1954. The plot – although not one of their best – demonstrates Galton and Simpson's ability to produce the scripted equivalent to a hall of mirrors. The reality of the first edition of *Hancock's Half Hour* is seen as a distorted, larger-than-life reflection; in time, even Hancock would find it increasingly difficult to recognise the fact from the comic fiction.

In the programme Hancock decided to throw a first-night party to celebrate the launch of his radio show. Assisted by Bill Kerr and Moira Lister, he searched for a more salubrious venue for his dinner party. Bill suggested an 'honest, upright, respectable, law-abiding member of the community' – smooth-talking Sid the estate agent.

When they arrived at Sid's recently opened office he was on the telephone, pressurising a client into renting a house. 'Now look, lady,' he said, 'I can't let you have the place any cheaper – four guineas a week and six hundred quid for the fittings. What do you mean what fittings? You've got running water? . . . Ah? . . . Well, put a bowl under it . . . Ah? . . . You want it decorated? . . . I'll send some balloons round, do it yourself.'

The exchange set the tone of Sid's character for the next six years.

CHAPTER SEVEN

Sid James was hitting the headlines. He was a West End star. He was in demand as a film actor. And he was fast becoming a much-loved member of an addictive radio comedy.

Although to Valerie family finances were still tight, their lifestyle was regularly attracting the attention of gossip columnists on the lookout for social glitz. Sid was enjoying his fame. Ray Galton and Alan Simpson were not far from the truth when they wrote a *Hancock's Half Hour* line for Sid expounding his philosophy on life: 'If you ain't got it, get it. When you've got it, spend it. Eat, drink, be merry – for tomorrow we snuff it.'

Unknown to Sid, his omnipotent presence on the stage, airwaves and cinema screens (ten films in 1954) had also caught the eye of the Inland Revenue. The books, as far as the Inspector of Taxes was concerned, did not balance. Sid would soon find himself on the brink of disaster. Other, more immediate, threats to his reputation he could control!

Sid still maintained contact with his mother, by now into her seventies. Reine's health was failing. Soon she would need constant care. In the way of most Jewish families the responsibility for ageing parents had fallen to the most successful and wealthiest son. Sid wrote to his cousin Joel Cohen saying he was 'in terrible trouble with his mother'. Cohen was a consultant gynaecologist for the Jewish Old Age Homes in Johannesburg. Through his influence he was able to add Reine James to the list of residents.

A year later, far from finding his cousin grateful, Joel Cohen discovered himself the victim of Sid's selective – and ruthless – amnesia.

Sid had brought down the shutters on his South African

years. It was as final and frightening as the slamming of a dungeon door. What light he allowed in depended on the memories his associates and relatives brought with them to England. Hidden firmly in the darkest corner were those who knew of Sid's lecherous and drunken exploits in the decade before the war. A family friend, who had witnessed his Halebron debut as Prince Charming but had not seen him since his teenage years, received the full James hospitality; his daughter, Elizabeth James, had been kept firmly at arm's length. A Johannesburg drinking friend on holiday in London had left a stage door message for Sid after watching him in *Guys and Dolls*. It was never answered. When he managed to make contact on the telephone, 'Sid was polite but made it quite obvious he had no intention of meeting.'

One of those whom Sid considered the greatest threat was Joel Cohen. 'I came to London on a number of occasions,' he recalls. 'Whenever I telephoned the theatres I was not allowed to speak to Sid. I was told, quite forcefully, that Sid did not want to re-establish contact with anyone from South Africa.' Cohen is convinced that Sid wanted to keep the first thirty-three years of his life 'a complete mystery'.

Not that Sid had much time to worry about his past life. November 1954 was proving a hectic month for him. In addition to his new commitment to *Hancock's Half Hour*, he was still appearing daily in *Guys and Dolls*. To capitalise on its success, Jack Hylton had decided the musical should tour a succession of suburban London venues such as Streatham Hill Theatre and the Golders Green Hippodrome. Sid still found time to take on more film work, this time Group Three's comedy *John and Julie*.

When the *Guys and Dolls* run ended in late November, Sid immediately began rehearsals for Jack Hylton's new musical *Wonderful Town*. His character would be known as 'The Wreck', an ex-champion footballer who spends his days as the general factotum in his wife's boarding house. Also starring Pat Kirkwood, the musical was a renamed and

101

re-vamped production of the American Broadway hit, *My Sister Eileen*. The show opened at Oxford on 13 December with a six-week Christmas season at Manchester and the London presentation already booked for Her Majesty's Theatre. Sid had also accepted the part of a night club gangster in the film *The Booby Trap*. Each week until the middle of February, Sid would return to London for the rehearsal and recording of *Hancock's Half Hour*.

The first radio series had lasted sixteen weeks. It ended, as it had begun, with an introspective script dealing with the programme and its cast. In the first, Hancock had thrown a party to celebrate his new show. In the final episode – broadcast on 15 February 1955 – Galton and Simpson decided to end with Hancock, Bill, Sid and Moira reminiscing on how they had met.

Verdicts on the series were mixed. Hancock, as ever, was nervous and felt it could have been better. Bill Kerr remained uncommitted. Sid, despite his initial hesitation, had enjoyed the experience. The BBC executives, and Dennis Main Wilson in particular, thought the series had 'gone rather well'.

Audience reaction to *Hancock's Half Hour* was mixed and misleading. Most listeners had enjoyed the new-style weekly comedy. Sid was the first to receive a practical demonstration of just how dramatically it had changed his life. Exactly eight days after the final BBC broadcast, Sid crowned the successful tour of *Wonderful Town* with its London debut. As he strode on to the Prince's Theatre stage the audience erupted, forcing a three-minute halt to the musical. His main number, 'Pass the Football', was accompanied by rhythmic handclapping and cheering.

The BBC quickly announced a second Hancock series. It would start just two months after the first and would be repeated on Sunday afternoons. During the twelve-week *Half Hour* run Sid would still be appearing at the Prince's Theatre in *Wonderful Town*. Because Sid had agreed to an option on a second series before signing his contract with Jack Hylton, the BBC still had first call on his services.

Hylton, for his part, did not want to open a new show with Sid James only to change the star halfway through its expected run. To head off any possible wrangle – and to allow Sid to appear in *Wonderful Town* – Dennis Main Wilson agreed the recording of any second Hancock series should be brought forward from its traditional Saturday evening slot to midday on Saturday. Hylton, for his part, agreed Sid would be released from the matinée performance.

It took just three months for Hancock's manic personality to infect the British people. By January 1955, *Hancock's Half Hour* was required listening for ten per cent of the population. Theatre managers and public house and chip shop owners were complaining the show was affecting their takings.

Part of Hancock's eternal fascination was that his character never ceased to reveal yet one more larger-than-life quirk or foible. Throughout the radio and television series Galton and Simpson would first create and then remould Hancock's imaginary ego and ancestry. In 1954 the 'shrewd, cunning, high-powered mug' was still a stranger. Only with hindsight is it possible to catalogue the 'complete' Hancock. In his book, *Hancock Artiste*, Roger Wilmut provides the best description of 'The Lad Himself'.

'Anthony Aloysius St John Hancock II, of 23 Railway Cuttings, East Cheam; dressed in a Homburg hat and a heavy overcoat with an astrakhan collar of uncertain age; a failed Shakespearean actor with pretensions of a knighthood and no books; age – 30s but claims to be younger; success with women – nil; financial success – nil; a pretentious, gullible, bombastic, occasionally kindly, superstitious, avaricious, petulant, over-imaginative, semi-educated, gourmandising, incompetent, cunning, obstinate, self-opinionated, impolite, pompous, lecherous, lonely and likeable fall-guy.'

Although Sid readily acknowledged Hancock's comic genius he was, at this stage, unaware of the fragile nature of Hancock's confidence. Success to Hancock was as brittle and bewildering as his popularity. When it approached, he withdrew. When it threatened to embrace him and make him a star, Hancock was afraid he might betray its trust. He had turned the *Talk of the Town* into a sell-out. Millions were tuning in to his radio programme. There was even rumour of a commercial television series to be written by Eric Sykes. Hancock fled, leaving the *Half Hour* team to pick up the pieces.

Dennis Main Wilson had called with a script at the Adelphi Theatre, where Hancock was appearing in *Talk of the Town*, only to be told Hancock had left before the finale. Accompanied by Jimmy Edwards, the producer toured every West End night club expecting to find Hancock drunk and repentant. But soon after 2.00 a.m. Main Wilson received a telephone call from a friend in the Special Branch. Hancock, he was informed, had been spotted at London Airport boarding a flight for Rome.

When Sid arrived at the studio for the week's rehearsal and recording he found Harry Secombe had been recruited to stand in for the absent star.

The show was recorded and transmitted with Secombe reading Hancock's lines. Main Wilson, under pressure from his superiors at the BBC, persuaded his police contact to enlist the help of Interpol. Hancock was eventually traced to a pensione in Positano. He refused to return until the first week in May 1955, by which time Secombe had appeared in the first three shows of the second series. When Hancock finally reappeared, Main Wilson recalls, he looked and acted 'like a little dog with his tail between his legs'.

Throughout the drama of Hancock's disappearance Sid had continued his nightly performances in *Wonderful Town*. The fourth *Half Hour* in the series was broadcast on 10 May, this time with Secombe making a 'farewell' guest appearance. At the exact moment the Hancock theme was hitting the airwaves Sid almost needed a stand-in of his own.

Racing off stage as the curtain came down for an interval, Sid tripped and collided head first with a stone proscenium.

He was unconscious for three minutes. The audience at the Prince's Theatre knew nothing of the backstage panic. Wobbly, and with a hastily camouflaged bump on his forehead, Sid insisted on resuming his part in the musical after the interval.

In 1955 the Inland Revenue finally caught up with Sid. What they found was nothing short of financial suicide.

Technically Sid was bankrupt. Tax returns from his early years in England had been forgotten. Demands for payment were ignored. Even with the belated intervention of an accountant Sid still owed more than £10,000 in back taxes. To salvage the situation and avoid possible court action, the Collector of Taxes offered Sid an escape route. The BBC and other film companies would pay Sid's fees direct to the Inland Revenue. It, in turn, would refund the Jameses enough to live on.

Like all gamblers, Sid was convinced 'one good killing' would salvage the situation. But instead of galloping past the winning post at 35 m.p.h. Sid's 'winner' turned out to be one of the slowest creatures on earth.

Sid was contacted by the director Carol Reed and asked if he would like a part in Reed's latest film. Adapted from the Max Catto novel, *The Killing Frost*, it was to be set in Paris and retitled *Trapeze*. Burt Lancaster, Tony Curtis and Gina Lollobrigida had already been signed for the leads. Coincidentally, Sid's first noteworthy performance with the Johannesburg Rep had been in the Max Catto play *They Walk Alone*.

Reed's timing was immaculate. With the money Sid was being offered for *Trapeze* he could pay off the tax man, reclaim his earnings and still have a little left over for a few weeks gambling.

There was only one problem. Sid's 'co-star' was to be a six-foot python. Sid's contract demanded he undergo a snake allergy test to ensure he would suffer no ill effects from handling the reptile. The only reaction snakes produced in Sid was fear. The mere thought of snakes brought him out in a sweat. If Sid had one pathological hatred in his life, it was for snakes. Faced with befriending the tax man or a snake, he opted for the reptile.

Sid arranged with Reed to borrow the python and, for six weeks, lived with it coiled around his neck or dozing in his lap. Sid arrived for his first day's shooting with his phobia at least under control. *Trapeze* was a circus drama. Sid's antics with the python left the camera crew in hysterics and Reed wondering whether he was directing the first *Goon Show*, an anarchic hit comedy of the time.

Sid would be placed in shot with the snake wrapped around his neck. What he had not been warned about was its tendency to doze off under the warm studio lights. As the python slept its muscles contracted; Sid was in danger of being strangled. The more he wrestled to free himself the more the snake tightened its grip. 'Help, help,' shouted Sid, his face wrapped in snake. 'This fucking thing's trying to murder me.' The cure was pure farce. Hearing Sid's muffled screams the trainer would rush on to the set, grab the last six inches of the snake's tail and slap it several times with the palm of his hand. It was, Reed was assured, the only way to save the life of his actor.

Sid's role of a one-time snake charmer attempting to sell his python because of an allergy is little more than that of a talking extra. In total he is in shot for less than five minutes. The snake enjoys more screen time than its 'owner'.

Trapeze was Sid's second film of the year for Carol Reed. In the spring of 1955 he had returned to Petticoat Lane and the Bishopsgate streets his grandparents had inhabited more than half a century earlier.

A Kid for Two Farthings was a whimsical comedy-drama written by Wolf Mankowitz and directed by Reed. Among the colourful market characters (Sid played 'Iceberg'), moves a boy whose pet goat appears to possess the magical power of a unicorn. The film's star was a young Diana Dors, whose life Sid would save several years later.

Trapeze was to be Sid's last film with the veteran director.

But fate would link them one final time. Sir Carol Reed and Sid James both died on the same day – 26 April 1976.

But, with the completion of *Trapeze*, Sid was happy. For the first time in months he was free to concentrate on what really mattered – attempting to beat the odds. It was an obsession which Valerie quickly confronted and, in her unique way, learned to deal with.

'I'd known about his gambling from the beginning, but I dismissed it from my mind,' Valerie says. 'To tell the truth, I think I loved him so much I didn't think it was important.'

Valerie knew to the penny how much the family needed to live on. She said that 'Sid asked me to look after the finances'. She would pay the day-to-day bills and Sid would be handed £5 a week 'pocket money'. To his friends Sid did little to dispel the image of a naughty schoolboy paying the price for past extravagances. The role was not totally out of character. Devising secret scams and backhanders to top up his pocket appealed as much to the schemer in Sid's make-up as the gambling did to the lifelong chancer.

In his controversial autobiography *No People Like Show People*, Michael Sullivan, Sid's future agent, claimed: 'Sidney accepted these restraints with a surprising equanimity. He played the good, dutiful husband to perfection.'

From then on Sid used his wife's 'stranglehold' on his cash as an excuse to cheat his friends, first out of their loyalty and, as his gambling debts grew bigger and his creditors more pressing, out of their money. To Sid it was all a game. To his friends – conned into keeping his escapades a secret – it was deadly serious.

Not long into the weekly recordings of *Hancock's Half Hour* Ray Galton and Alan Simpson noticed that Sid would often slip away during a quiet moment in rehearsals. He would be found hiding his face behind a hand as he mumbled bets into a telephone.

Most of the actors and actresses employed on the comedy series were older than the writers who, recalls Ray Galton, were generally referred to as 'the boys'. Social excursions between cast and writers were rare. On one occasion Sid suggested an evening 'at the dogs'. Galton and Simpson, and their wives, joined Sid and Val and Hancock and his wife Cicely at Wembley Greyhound Stadium. Val, as ever, appeared 'slim and lady-like, elegant and rather cool'.

Early in the evening Sid called Alan Simpson aside. 'Look,' he whispered to the writer, 'I've told Val I've cut the betting down.' As ever, Sid had a scheme. Before each race Sid would announce to the group which dogs he was backing. He would then slip Simpson a handful of £10 notes. Sid, dutifully watched by Val, would make his way to the two-shilling betting window while Simpson, primed with Sid's selection, would place the real bets elsewhere. 'He would come back with his tickets and show them to Val while I had all his heavy bets,' recalls Simpson. 'If his bets came up I had to make an excuse to go outside to collect the money and slide his winnings to him.'

As ever, Val knew what was going on. 'That was one of our things, neither of us pressurised the other into doing anything we didn't want to do. If you have someone who says you can't do this or that, you end up wanting to do it even more. That's why I never tried to stop him gambling – I knew he needed it. Gambling was like breathing to Sid – second nature.'

It didn't help that directors and producers saw Sid as the obligatory wide-boy. Late in 1955, Maurice Elvey, hired to direct a screen version of the long-running Brian Rix stage farce *Dry Rot*, threatened to pull out of the project unless his gang of bumbling bookmakers included Sid James. On the set Sid impressed a 25-year-old actress for an entirely different reason.

Joan Sims, who was also to become a *Carry On* regular, watched the autocratic Elvey's rising blood pressure with alarm. The target of the director's frustration was actor Michael Shepley who, for some reason, found it impossible to co-ordinate his split-second series of entries and exits – a trademark of any Brian Rix farce. 'Oh, do come along,' bellowed Elvey after thirty minutes of re-takes. 'We must get this right.'

Sid's face tightened. 'That was inexcusable,' he informed the director. 'Until you apologise to Michael for that outburst, I'm off.' The cast and crew watched open-mouthed as Sid strode off the set. 'I was hugely impressed by the stand Sid took for his fellow actor,' admitted Joan Sims.

Sid's sense of superstition was now being reinforced by coincidence. But although he felt he could manipulate his luck – he once touched wood no less than thirty-nine times during one newspaper interview – Sid had far better results with fate. One manifestation, which would last throughout his career, was the intriguing and unexplained habit of television and film subjects to arrive in pairs: in 1962 the films *We Joined the Navy* and *Carry On Cruising*; in 1963, *Carry On Cabby* and the television series *Taxi*. By 1955 the trend was already established. *A Kid for Two Farthings* was swiftly followed by a second film set around the adventures of children.

Part of Group Three's entertainment (if not financial) success was that it plugged into common British experiences. *Orders Are Orders* – like the first *Carry On* film five years later – relied on National Service. Sid's fourth and final film for the company used the mystery and pomp of the Coronation. Actually filmed in 1955, two years after the event, *John and Julie* tells the story of a brother and sister running away from home to see Elizabeth II crowned. The film, in which Sid plays the obnoxious step-father Mr Pritchett, not only reunited him with Peter Sellers but also allowed him to make his one and only film with Moira Lister.

The New Year started with a perfect partnership. But Sid soon discovered he had landed himself a small part in a long-running disaster.

Late in 1955 Sid had been approached through his agent about a part in a British-financed picture starring Bob Hope and Katharine Hepburn. The film would be produced by Betty E. Box but was being masterminded by the veteran comedian from across the Atlantic. The film, written as *Not for Money*, involved a US Air Force officer falling in love during the Cold War with a beautiful but dedicated Communist. The publicity – and political – opportunities were too good to ignore. Hope announced he wanted to shoot the comedy behind the Iron Curtain and Box set about approaching the Soviet authorities. The answer, not unexpectedly, was a suspicious no.

But it was the screenplay which caused most of the problems. The lead had originally been offered to Cary Grant. He backed out within days of reading Ben Hecht's script. As replacement Hope soon clashed with Hecht, who was more of a craftsman writer than the punch-line automaton Hope demanded. The comedian and writer were soon slugging it out line by line and Hecht quit, demanding his name was removed from all credits and that he should in no way be associated with the project. Hope unleashed his platoon of gag writers on the script, who promptly renamed it *The Iron Petticoat*.

Shooting – or at least Sid's part of it – began at Pinewood in January 1956. Director Ralph Thomas charmed the press by saying: 'It wouldn't be a British picture if it didn't have Sidney James in it.'

When it appeared later in the year the film flopped. Even the pairing of Hope and Hepburn failed to win over the critics, who called it a watery imitation of *Ninotchka*, the hilarious Greta Garbo pre-war comedy on the same theme.

After the near disaster of the previous year Valerie was determined she was not going to be faced with the taxman's ultimatum a second time. In the spring of 1956 she formed a limited company – James (Arts) Ltd – with herself and her accountant as sole directors. Sid was not even listed as a shareholder. In April, the BBC accounts department was informed that all future contracts should be made out to James (Arts) Ltd, with payments made direct to Archie Parnell and Co. The first BBC contract issued to James (Arts) Ltd was for Sid's part in a *Saturday Night Theatre* radio production of *The Volunteer*, for which the company was paid thirty guineas.

The Inland Revenue was not the only body attempting to retrieve money from Sid James. One unexpected demand came from the South African government. It had recently decided that all overseas training grants given to former servicemen should now be repaid. Sid and Meg had used the £450 to travel to England. Those in ordinary employment were allowed to pay weekly. High-profile ex-servicemen, like Sid and Laurence Harvey, were expected to settle the debt outright.

In the 1960s Sid renounced his South African citizenship and became a British national. He was, he felt, still a South African. 'I root for the boys when they come over here with the sports team. I still feel one of them.' The change, he said, was more to do with his need to travel. 'It had nothing to do with the republic or apartheid. But I had such a bother trying to get visas when I wanted to go into other countries that a British passport was more helpful.'

Life in the Lymington Road apartment was becoming even more hectic. One feature was earning international press coverage. Sid's bar – which occupied a complete room of the Hampstead flat – consisted of plain white-wood furniture and wall-to-wall deep scarlet carpet. Its walls were covered in just two kinds of decoration – a cluster of framed photographs of Sid in his film and stage roles, and scores of miniature liquor bottles. The shelves, as Sid informed any new guest, he had built himself.

The permanent occupants of the flat included the couple's son, Stephen, born in February 1954, a maid, and a boxer dog called Buster. Other, temporary, visitors included Gene Kelly, Vivian Blaine, Robert Taylor and Kay Kendall.

One person who rarely called was Tony Hancock. His own Queen's Gate Terrace apartment, a short walk from the Albert Hall and Hyde Park, was seedy in comparison to Sid's. He may have enjoyed – even sought – the company of Sid's guests, but the reality of his own existence was aggravatingly slummy compared to the Jameses' apparently well-ordered and prosperous lifestyle. In the biography

111

Hancock, Dennis Main Wilson recalls a visit to Tony and Cicely's fifth-floor home: 'There was an old leather club armchair with the stuffing coming out, a few other odd chairs and a Put-U-Up settee. There was an underfelt on the floor but no carpet. There was a mark where someone had been sick. There were piles of fan letters behind the lavatory pan. I looked into the bedroom one Sunday and there was a *Sunday Pictorial* from the previous week still sticking out of the bedclothes.'

Both men were living a lie. Hancock, who for the first time in his career was earning a star's salary, was returning to a home little better than a slum. Sid, whose plush surroundings reflected his growing status, was struggling to finance his apparently suicidal urge to gamble.

Yet it was Hancock who, in his attempt to make sense of his existence and his place in mankind as a whole, began to doubt his own importance. 'But it's the money that worries me,' Hancock once told Kenneth Williams. 'Look at the vast sums they're paying me for this series and think what that bus driver gets.' It was a doubt which never troubled Sid. While Hancock studied Bertrand Russell's *History of Western Philosophy* and Kant's *Critique of Pure Reason*, Sid read the *Sporting Life* and evaluated the favourite's chances in the two-thirty at Fontwell.

Ray Galton explains: 'It wasn't so much the crookedness of Sid we used but his earthy realism, as opposed to Hancock's phoney artistry. Hancock pretended to know about opera and art, whereas to Sid if it was not horse racing it was of no interest.' He was speaking of Sid's *Half Hour* persona. He might equally have been describing Sid James the actor.

Once again it was Valerie who took control. The family needed a bigger and more permanent home. They found it at 35 Gunnersbury Avenue, Ealing. Val set about decorating the bay-fronted house to her own 'plush and royal' standards. The four bedrooms provided enough room to accommodate any guests and the one-hundred-foot garden was big enough for Stephen to play in safely. Sid liked it because it was only a short drive from the White City dog track.

The Jameses' move to west London enacted a subtle change on Sid's relationship with his daughter, Reine. Somehow, she remembers, contact with her father became 'less frequent and more perfunctory'. Two years earlier, in 1954, Meg and her daughter had left Allan House for a new home in Chelsea's Royal Hospital Road. Sid had still found time to call in unannounced. Nine-year-old Reine suddenly became aware it was she who was the 'visitor – the outsider'.

'Our meetings were no longer of him to me,' she recalls. 'They were always at an aforementioned place. I would be taken in the car. It would always be me visiting him. I would go to the new family home and have lunch; very rarely would I see him on his own. Sometimes it would be in his dressing room, just to say hello.'

The company accounts were soon showing a healthy profit. Early in June 1956, Sid had signed two contracts with the BBC: one for the first television series of *Hancock's Half Hour*, the second for a new radio series with Peter Sellers entitled *Finkel's Caff*. Both would run throughout July and August and into September, allowing Sid very little free time between rehearsals and the live television transmissions and the radio recordings. The three months – although not totally successful – proved a landmark in Sid's career. For the first time he would have the unique distinction of appearing on both radio and television with two of the country's biggest stars.

Six years earlier, in March 1950, Peter Sellers had teamed up with Miriam Karlin to broadcast *Sellers' Market*. The pair, who shared a passion for mimicry and funny voices, played two East End stall-holders and their numerous idiosyncratic patrons. The series lasted for only six shows. An attempt, six years later, to revive the format – this time with Sid replacing Karlin – was equally doomed.

Two days before television viewers caught their first glimpse of Hancock the comic actor, listeners to the Light Programme were allowed through the doors of *Finkel's Caff*

– 'where the elite meet to eat'. The first programme was broadcast at 8.30 p.m. on 4 July. As part of Sid's contract for the nine shows the BBC had included the option to engage Sid for a further three. In the event only one additional programme was made.

All ten open to the same tinkling bar-room piano. 'The sound of that battered piano heralds your weekly visit to *Finkel's Caff.* When you get to Soho, turn right, go past the second-hand clothes shop, past the stall selling cut-price cosmetics, past the Gents Haircut-and-Shave and there – right next door to the Pin Table Arcade – that restaurant is *Finkel's Caff . . .*' The proprietor, Finkel, never makes an appearance. His café is managed by Peter Sellers as Irishman Eddie.

Sid's earning potential from the new series was considerable. Unlike the radio series of *Hancock's Half Hour,* which the BBC rated as 'domestic' comedy, each episode of *Finkel's Caff* was scheduled for three separate overseas transmissions. In addition to the initial fee of thirty guineas, Sid – or rather James (Arts) Ltd – received an extra eighteen guineas for each programme. Such was the pulling power of a Frank Muir and Denis Norden script, fronted by Peter Sellers and supported by Sid James, Kenneth Connor and Avril Angers.

The public, and ultimately the BBC, disagreed. The series was axed after ten weeks. No recordings and only two scripts have survived.

Early in 1956, a BBC radio audience research report reflected the public's growing acceptance of the *Half Hour* stalwarts as an inter-dependent team. Hancock ranked equally with Sid and Kenneth Williams. It was a view which did not please Hancock. He had no wish to be part of a great comedy team – any comedy team for that matter.

A solution to Hancock's frustration was only a few weeks away. The BBC announced it was time for *Hancock's Half Hour* to make the inevitable move to television. There were numerous benefits for Hancock, not the least of which was a significant increase in his earning potential. Very soon he would be the first man on British television to be paid £1,000 for a thirty-minute programme, even though it involved a full week's work.

Hancock also made no secret of his intention to use his television show to break new ground, part of which was the destruction of the old partnership. Duncan Wood, the show's producer, was left in no doubt that Hancock saw his success primarily as a solo performer, a view strangely at odds with his earlier pronouncement to Dennis Main Wilson that 'the show is the thing; only the show matters'. Bill Kerr was dropped altogether and Kenneth Williams only reappeared for the six programmes of the second television series. Only Sid, whom Hancock considered his greatest threat, was to remain. From the start he repeatedly told Galton and Simpson, retained to write the TV scripts, that: 'I don't want this to develop into a double act.'

Year by year the viewers came to disagree with Hancock. The first television *Half Hour* was broadcast on 6 July 1956. Sid, who by now had completed fifty films, as opposed to Hancock's one, felt the most comfortable in front of the cameras and lights. From the start his performances were less self-conscious and more relaxed than Hancock's.

Although many fans were disappointed, the viewing figures were nonetheless respectable. Sixteen per cent of the adult population of Britain switched on to watch – the equivalent of thirty-six per cent of the TV-owning public. Eight months later the viewing figure had risen to twenty-three per cent, a full twelve points above what the BBC accepted as respectable for a light entertainment programme. By November 1959 it had topped twenty-seven per cent. And in March 1960 – the final survey before Sid's departure – twenty-eight per cent of the population regularly sat down to watch *Hancock's Half Hour*.

As the figures rose, so did Sid's popularity. Survey sheets began to record the depth to which viewers had adopted the fellow resident of 23 Railway Cuttings. Phrases such as, 'A *Hancock's Half Hour* without Sid is as unthinkable as one without Hancock,' and, 'Tony Hancock would not be the same without Sidney James,' began to appear on the questionnaires. The BBC management thought it wise not to allow Hancock to see the comments.

The fourth radio series of *Hancock's Half Hour* started its run on 14 October 1956 and continued weekly until the end of February 1957. One notable addition to the cast was Hattie Jacques, having worked as Hancock's foil as the over-amorous Agatha Dinglebody in *Educating Archie*. This time she would portray the outsize, incompetent, aggressive Grizelda Pugh whom Hancock hires as a secretary. It was the first time Sid had worked with Jacques. They remained close friends until Sid's death. As well as being a *Carry On* stalwart – she appeared in fourteen films – Jacques is best remembered for her long-running BBC partnership with Eric Sykes.

Having started the year at least appearing in the same film as Hope and Hepburn, the autumn brought Sid the chance to play opposite one of the comedy legends of all time – Charlie Chaplin. *A King in New York*, filmed at Shepperton Studios near London, was one of eight films Sid appeared in and released the following year.

In the film Sid was cast as a high-pressure American salesman who has something to sell to Chaplin, playing the king. The role not only pleased, but also suited Sid, who enjoyed getting his tongue and ability around an American character. 'Going on with a legend was a terrific challenge,' confessed Sid, 'but I let him have it.'

The second fortnightly television series of *Hancock's Half Hour* began on 1 April 1957. Sid would miss the first two of the six-episode series. He was invited by the *Radio Times* – through the imagination of Galton and Simpson – to expound on *My Boy Hancock*:

> *I have been asked to contribute four hundred words on my impressions of Tony Hancock. This is going to be very difficult on account of I don't know four hundred words. But I shall have a go and try not to repeat too many times the ones I do know.*

I first met Tony Hancock on the railway line that runs past Wandsworth prison. I'd just finished the long climb down the wall, and he was trying to thumb a lift to Brighton. From that day we have been inseparable. Not because I like him, but with what he knows about me I daren't let him out of my sight.

What were my first impressions of him as we stood facing each other across the sleepers? He appeared to be a podgy, seedy little man, in a shabby suit, going a bit green across the shoulders, his shirt collar slightly frayed, a faded Royal Air Force tie, and grubby spats only partly hiding a pair of elastic-sided boots, right down at the heel. There, I thought to myself, is a man who's seen better days. Afterwards I found out I was wrong. He hadn't seen better days; he'd always been that way. However, he took a liking to me and pledging our everlasting trust in each other, we shook hands and two days later I sold him his wristwatch back.

Hancock is now one of the highest paid comedians in Britain. He doesn't know this, of course, because I am also his agent. I am not frightened about him reading this, as I also happen to be his publicity agent, and advise him on what, and what not, to read. And on top of that there's what I cop from being in his radio and television shows, his personal manager, financial adviser, income-tax consultant and landlord, so you can see why I'm not particularly worried about the increase in the Bank Rate.

Finally I would like to thank the BBC and members of the public for the continued interest in my boy, and I hope they will enjoy this new series on television as much as I'm going to enjoy banking my nineteen and six out of every pound he makes.

What Sid was 'copping' from the Hancock comedies was considerable. A twenty-week run of radio programmes – the fourth radio series – ended on 24 February 1957. Sid's fee for each programme, excluding repeats, was forty-five guineas. Work on the second television series began almost immediately, with transmission just thirty-five days later on 1 April. For these Sid received one hundred guineas per show. The public response to the early episodes was so great that the BBC immediately commissioned a third TV series. This time the twelve programmes would be transmitted weekly, starting on 30 September 1957, with the final episode (on 23 December) scheduled to give the BBC a headstart in the Christmas ratings war.

Sid had been absent from two television *Half Hour*s. He had no intention of missing a third – not even for the birth of a daughter. Susan Valerie James was born at Queen Charlotte's Hospital, Hammersmith, on Monday, 7 October 1957. That night her father returned to the BBC studio for a live transmission of *Hancock's Half Hour*. Sid was forty-four years old. He had become a father for the seventh time. Within six months he would become a grandfather.

Elizabeth James – whom Sid had not seen since her visit to England – had married Benny Grevler. The couple were now living in Bulawayo, Southern Rhodesia. Despite an invitation to the wedding, Sid had claimed he was too busy to attend. When Elizabeth discovered she was pregnant she broke the good news to her father in a letter. Sid never wrote back. His granddaughter, Suzzane, was born early in 1958.

Just before Christmas 1957, Tony Hancock was voted Comedian of the Year by the Guild of Television Producers and Directors. Other television series in which Sid was involved, though, were less successful. That year Sid had wrapped a handkerchief around his head and donned a leather jerkin to become a pirate. He joined the crew of *The Buccaneers* as the lute-playing Shanty Jack – 'forty-one years on the sea'. The derring-do series was the corporation's home-grown answer to the flood of western adventures from America. The BBC chose Robert Shaw as its high seas hero, Captain Dan Tempest. Among the cast was Joan Sims who, two years earlier, had worked with Sid on *Dry Rot*.

Hancock, however, celebrated his new status as Britain's top comedian by selling his apartment in Queen's Gate

Terrace and buying a house in Lingfield, Surrey. He renamed it MacConkeys after its original owner.

Among the regular guests were Sid and Valerie. Hancock, they noticed, was drinking more heavily than ever. Through the haze, Hancock first distilled and then poured his own philosophy of his and Sid's art. 'Comedy,' Hancock would often tell his guests, 'is frustration, misery, boredom, worry – all the things people suffer from.'

It had been obvious to everyone, and not just the guests at MacConkeys, that Hancock had also been 'suffering' for some time.

Each week Duncan Wood presided over rehearsals for the television *Half Hours*. The weekly sessions were attended by Galton and Simpson and held in a boys' club the BBC had hired in Sulgrave Road, not far from its Shepherd's Bush studios.

It was here, among the ping-pong and snooker tables, and with the air smelling of sawdust and damp coconut matting, that Hancock subconsciously worked some of his most precious magic. It was here, too, that some of the gnawing doubts over his talent began to nibble away at his confidence. Hancock used the unhurried and informal atmosphere of the rehearsals more and more as a protective smoke-screen.

'We would arrive around ten-thirty and have a cup of coffee and a game of snooker,' Sid recalled. 'After a brief run-through we would play snooker or table tennis for a couple of hours and then go to lunch.' Two hours later the cast and crew would reassemble. 'We would have another game of table tennis and do another couple of hours' rehearsal. By this time it would be about six o'clock and the boys would start to gather for the opening of the club.'

As Sid prepared to go, Hancock would announce: 'Can we go over this line once more? I don't think we have got it right yet.'

The radio series of *Hancock's Half Hour* continued with a life of its own. Despite his initial hesitation Sid was still enjoying the experience. Dennis Main Wilson, who had persuaded Sid to 'try his hand at radio comedy', left in February 1957, at the end of the fourth series. He had overseen the production of sixty-eight shows. Main Wilson remembers Sid as a 'truly professional actor, who happened to look as tough and evil as a prize fighter'.

Only once did Sid live up to his image. It was also the only time he was late for work. Sid was in a black London cab on his way to a *Half Hour* rehearsal. The taxi was following a three-wheeled Robin Reliant car being driven by an orthodox Jew with long curls and wearing a black hat. Every time the Reliant attempted to overtake a bus the taxi driver pulled alongside the three-wheeler, blocking the road and sounding his horn. The cabby slid back his glass screen and announced: 'I hate bloody Jews, don't you?'

Sid ordered the taxi driver to stop. As the cab pulled up Sid leaped out and yanked open the driver's door. The cabby, sensing what was about to happen, lashed out with his foot. Before the boot made contact Sid landed one blow, knocking the cabby over the bonnet and into the road.

CHAPTER EIGHT

On 9 January 1958, Tom Sloan, head of light entertainment at BBC Television, had the uncomfortable experience of learning from the morning newspapers that the co-star of his most successful comedy series had been poached by his independent rivals.

Sid James, as most of the morning papers announced, had been signed for a new six-part series by Associated Rediffusion. The script had been written by Wolf Mankowitz, and Sid would star alongside Miriam Karlin. Negotiations had been kept so secret that the series – called *East End, West End* – was unveiled only after the first programme had been given a transmission slot on 4 February.

Associated Rediffusion had scored a major publicity victory over the BBC. By exploiting Sid's considerable popularity it looked set to challenge Tony Hancock's television ratings head on. The BBC was also faced with the situation of having six radio editions of the fifth *Hancock's Half Hour* series – in which Sid played a leading part – broadcast on the same day each week as independent television's *East End, West End*.

If Mankowitz had not exactly copied Sid's *Half Hour* persona – itself created by Galton and Simpson – he had certainly exploited the shadier side of Sid's East Cheam character. *East End, West End* was set amid London's Jewish community of big-time operators and small-time dealers. Sid uses his wits to keep him out of jail and turn a half-honest profit. The initial six-week run would end on 11 March. This, according to the press announcement, would be followed by a seven-week lay off, and a second series of thirteen programmes.

'I am sorry that we have not had the chance of doing this series on BBC,' Sloan wrote to Sid after studying the day's newspapers. 'But, as you have made your decision, my principal concern is safeguarding the Tony Hancock series which we will be starting in October.' Sloan was worried that additional option clauses on future *East End, West End* series might stop Sid rejoining Hancock. 'I would like you to take this letter as a firm indication of our desire to have you in that series in October.'

In the event Sloan need not have worried. *East End, West End* was axed by Associated Rediffusion after the first six programmes. Miriam Karlin's only comment on her one and only experience of working with Sid is that it was an idea 'ahead of its time'.

Early in September 1958, Sid and Valerie snatched their first proper holiday together for seven years. Other holidays had been planned, but they had always been cancelled because of Sid's paranoia about losing work. 'I don't refuse work,' he confessed on more than one occasion. 'I'd rather be grumbling about having too much work to take a holiday than having to take a holiday because there's not enough work.'

The couple flew to Nice for a week's break in the south of France. Sid had just finished work on *Make Mine a Million*, in which he and Arthur Askey use a mobile television transmitter to advertise detergent. Within days of his return he would be back at Pinewood Studios, this time for Mario Zampi's *Too Many Crooks*. Among the other actors to be on the set were Terry-Thomas, George Cole, and the 6ft 7in Bernard Bresslaw.

Sid had mixed views on two of the films he worked on that year. Both reminded him of his days with the South African Entertainment Unit. *Silent Enemy* told of the wartime exploits of Commander Buster Crabb. The Royal Navy frogman – who disappeared in 1956 while on an underwater spying mission in Portsmouth Harbour – was played by Laurence Harvey. The part of Chief Petty Officer Thorpe was offered to Sid on Harvey's suggestion. While

Sid always remembered the role as 'something special', he did not enjoy working with Harvey – by now a star in his own right. 'Sid thought Larry had risen too far and too fast,' explains their former colleague, Muff Evans. As the shooting came to an end Harvey made a loud and very public display of announcing that his professional debt to Sid had now been repaid. The incident irked Sid. 'By now Larry was pompous and full of his own importance, and Sid detested that. I don't think they ever spoke to each other again.'

In Basil Dearden's *Ensa Story*, eventually renamed and released as *Desert Mice*, Sid played broken-down comedian Bert Bennett, a member of an ENSA concert party touring the North African battlefront. Bennett's wife was played by Dora Bryan.

But there were some roles, equally suited to Sid's experience, which he refused to accept. Sid was offered the part of Archie Rice in a South African stage tour of *The Entertainer*. For years the play's lead had been dominated by Laurence Olivier's portrayal of the ageing vaudeville star. 'Although Archie's life was my life for years,' Sid admitted, 'although I have lived it, I couldn't hope to come anywhere near Olivier's performance.' Sid wrote back to the producer saying he 'wouldn't dare' take the part.

The BBC was determined not to let Sid James slip through its fingers a second time. Exactly a year after Associated Television had unveiled its ill-fated *East End, West End*, the corporation approached Phyllis Parnell about a series of its own.

Parnell discussed the suggestion with Sid before replying to Eric Maschwitz. The BBC's idea was to slot a series, written especially for Sid, between the end of the current run of the television *Hancock's Half Hour* on Good Friday and the start of a fifth Hancock TV series in September. Sid was against the idea because, as Parnell told Maschwitz, '. . . with an additional series in between he may be outstaying his television "welcome" '. Sid was also being 'overwhelmed' by film offers, added Parnell, many of which he wanted to accept '. . . particularly as one would mean a very nice few weeks on location in Spain'.

The 'Spanish' film Sid was reluctant to turn down was *Tommy the Toreador*, a vehicle film for pop singer Tommy Steele. The musical is based around a young British seaman who takes the place of a bullfighter framed for smuggling. Among the co-stars was Kenneth Williams. He had previously worked with Steele in a West End pantomime, and thought him 'very kind and good'.

Tommy the Toreador was also the second film within a year – there are only two – in which Sid worked with Bernard Cribbins. 'Sid was great to be with both on and off the set,' recalls Cribbins. In later years they shared a passion for both fishing and cricket. In Spain Cribbins had a hard job keeping up with Sid's determination to enjoy himself.

When filming at Elstree Studios was completed, the crew and the cast moved to Seville in Spain. On the final night, with the film safely in the can, Sid and Val invited Cribbins out for a meal. It quickly degenerated into a pub crawl and ended with ringside seats at an amateur boxing tournament. Between bouts Sid and Cribbins did their best to prop up both the bar and the Spanish distilling industry. Cribbins remembers little else of their night on the town except that 'Valerie had to look after us somewhat.'

One 1959 film offer was to change Sid's acting career for ever. In the late spring Parnell was approached to see if Sid would be interested in taking the lead in the fourth film of what had already become a popular and moneyspinning series of productions. He would go on to take part in nineteen *Carry On* films.

But Sid's invitation to join the *Carry On* crew was prompted more by politics than personal choice. Ted Ray, a music hall and radio comedian, had played the lead as the headmaster in the third of the series, *Carry On Teacher*. Peter Rogers, the producer, was happy with Ray's performance and had all but signed him for *Carry On Constable*.

During the late summer of 1959, Rogers was informed by Stuart Levy, boss of Anglo Amalgamated films, that he would have to drop Ray from the planned cast. Associated British – whose ABC cinemas screened the films – had apparently taken offence at Ray's successful appearance in *Teacher*. When Rogers pressed for an explanation he discovered that Ray had at one time been under contract to Associated British, but had never been given a film. At first the producer intended to stand his ground, but Levy pushed even harder. Without its own cinema chain, Anglo was reliant on the ABC network. If Rogers insisted on keeping Ted Ray, then Associated British would refuse to screen any more *Carry On*s.

Rogers broke the news to Ted Ray, carefully guarding the truth to avoid what he feared might trigger a lawsuit. To plug the gap, Rogers and director Gerald Thomas chose Sid James.

As Sergeant Frank Wilkins, it is Sid's job to run a flu-decimated police station while knocking three replacements into shape. The newcomers sent to try the long-suffering Sid are Leslie Phillips, Kenneth Williams and Kenneth Connor, as constables Potter, Benson and Constable. The film is basically a succession of quick-fire disasters as each rookie takes to the beat.

Shooting for *Carry On Constable* started on 9 November 1959, not at Pinewood Studios but in an empty Ealing property just a couple of miles from Sid's Gunnersbury Avenue home. Kenneth Williams – whose eternal disillusionment had already caused him to dub the film 'mediocre and tired' – recorded the scene in his diary: 'The location is a dreary house ... water dripping everywhere. Rain pouring down. Charming.'

Peter Rogers's ban on the reproduction of *Carry On* dialogue forbids the inclusion of the line which gave Sid his first ever laugh in a *Carry On* film. Written by Norman Hudis, it involves investigating suspicious goings-on at the rear-end of a local woman's property. This standard would remain basically the same for Sid's next eighteen *Carry On* films.

So, too, would Sid's friendship with fellow actor Kenneth Connor. Both men had worked together on the ill-fated *Finkel's Caff*. A very private person with a passion for football, Connor found a new confidence on the film set. His apparently off-the-cuff remarks would frequently crack up his colleagues. 'If I had to be locked up,' Sid once confessed, 'Kenneth would be one of my choices for a cell-mate.'

Sid donned a police uniform again during 1959, this time in the glossy but empty-headed comedy, *Upstairs and Downstairs*. Strangely out of touch for the late fifties, the plot – as the title suggests – centres on the domestic problems between newlyweds and their maids. One young actress who made her film debut in *Upstairs and Downstairs* was Susan James, Sid's eighteen-month-old daughter.

The film's director, Ralph Thomas, was keeping a tight rein on Sid's image. The action ends just as Sid announces he has married a female colleague and intends retiring from the force. 'There is no way I could allow Sid to walk down the aisle,' adds Thomas. 'The public would never believe it and besides that battered face just doesn't go with a romantic role.'

Another reunion proved just as profitable. Ronnie Wolfe had first met Sid at London's Mapleton Hotel in the early 1950s. Since then they had met briefly in the corridors of Broadcasting House or at various recording studios. Wolfe was co-writing, with Ronald Chesney and Marty Feldman, the script for a popular radio show. He suggested its new-season guest should be Sid James.

In the 1930s and 40s the Columbia Broadcasting System had demonstrated that a talking doll could capture equal ratings with its 'human' rivals. At one time, the *Edgar Bergen and Charlie McCarthy Show* was America's favourite light entertainment programme. It also had the dubious distinction of being the show during which millions of listeners habitually reached for their dials to avoid the regular singing spot. On 30 October 1938, they stumbled on Orson Welles' notorious dramatisation of *War of the Worlds* – and panicked.

Inspired by Charlie McCarthy, the BBC gave Archie Andrews – the eternal schoolboy – a shot at stardom. It lasted ten years. Throughout the 1950s *Educating Archie* remained one of the most popular shows on the radio. The combination of a mischievous, blazer-clad, wooden dummy – unseen by millions of listeners yet taking an active part in every broadcast – and Peter Brough's larynx, proved irresistible.

More importantly, the programme turned gifted, but relatively unknown, beginners into stars. Among the cast for the first series in 1950 was Julie Andrews as Archie's girlfriend. Most took their turn as Archie's tutor. One series, which started in August 1951, introduced Tony Hancock. By 1952 many fans rated Hancock as the comedy's real star. He was followed by Harry Secombe and, in later years, by Ronald Shiner (1953), Bernard Miles (1954), James Robertson Justice (1955), and Bruce Forsyth in 1959. The exception was Sid James. Already a household name through his association with Hancock and his numerous film roles, Sid agreed to join the cast, in December 1959, for an eight-week run as Archie's latest tutor.

It was Wolfe's first experience of working with Sid. 'He always showed a great, great respect for writers,' Wolfe recalls. 'He knew that in comedy you couldn't get anywhere without them, so he always gave the writers full credit.'

The trio of writers were also getting a few laughs at Sid's expense. In an early *Educating Archie* script Sid opens a newspaper. 'What's in the news? Russian dog shoots up into space at eighteen thousand miles per hour. My luck! Last night at the White City my dog wouldn't even leave the trap.'

Sid's 'studio professionalism' also impressed Wolfe,

whose book, *Writing Comedy*, has become one of the classic manuals for would-be scriptwriters. 'There was never any temperament from Sid. He was never greedy with laughs and he fed lines beautifully. And he was never like some other actors who demanded to know, "Why am I saying this? What is my motivation?" If a line worked, Sid made it funny.'

It soon became obvious that Sid was less honest about his gambling and his girlfriends. Wolfe remembers: 'The only time Sid got a bit touchy was when he had a lot of money on a dog or a horse and he had to rehearse. All he wanted to do was run to the telephone. His mind was on other things.'

The first time Wolfe was invited to Gunnersbury Avenue was for a lavish show-business party – 'the high-class rent-a-mob'. The house, he discovered, was decorated primarily in white. Valerie proved an 'exceptionally attractive and capable hostess'.

Wolfe was invited back to work on scripts or film ideas. The discussions were frequently interrupted while Sid played with an electric train, set out on the front-room floor, or disappeared upstairs to bathe one of the children.

Although it never led to any serious disagreement, Wolfe found it hard to square Sid's apparently genuine devotion to his wife and children with his numerous affairs. 'Sid never had any conscience about screwing around,' recalls the scriptwriter.

Away from Ealing, Sid expected – indeed, demanded – help from his colleagues in keeping his affairs a secret from Valerie. Not once did he thank his co-conspirators. Nor were Sid's connivings ever mentioned again. Sid would arrive at rehearsals to be handed a message to call someone. There was never any name. While the cast relaxed during a break Sid would make straight for the telephone. 'It was obvious he wasn't talking to his bookie,' recalls one fellow actor. 'Sometimes, late in the day, he would be called away to answer the phone. It was always a woman.'

To spend more time with his current lover Sid would enlist the assistance of most of the production staff in turn.

He needed an alibi for staying out late. Or, once or twice a month, an excuse to spend a Saturday afternoon and evening away from home.

The first time, Wolfe thought it was an 'elaborate gag'. Sid had primed the writer to telephone on Saturday morning. 'I should have got a drama award for my performance,' Wolfe admits. 'I heard myself saying: "You've got to come, Sid. You must. Your career is more important than anything else." ' Reluctantly Sid would be persuaded to attend the special rehearsal – 'for the good of the show'.

Wolfe is also convinced that Val, as a former actress, would have known exactly what was going on. 'Anyone in their right mind knew what was happening,' he adds. 'If you are doing a show on Sunday you don't call a rehearsal on Saturday night. By that time the script is either right or it isn't.'

Late in the autumn of 1959, Tony Hancock called a meeting at MacConkeys, his five-bedroomed house in the Surrey countryside north of East Grinstead. Among those present were Ray Galton and Alan Simpson, and his television producer Duncan Wood. Sid James was not invited.

Everyone knew what was coming. Hancock told them he was bored and frustrated with the pompous character in the Homburg hat and the confined world he inhabited at 23 Railway Cuttings. The set was too dowdy and parochial. Sid's Cockney accent was irritating. Above all, Hancock wanted international recognition. At the end of one heavy silence, during which the trio looked at each other like schoolboys in the middle of a dressing down, Hancock announced the end of *Hancock's Half Hour*. And then, as if he realised he had gone too far, Hancock backed down. He would do one more series – but only if they agreed to move him out of East Cheam and away from Sid.

'We went along with him,' the scriptwriters recall, 'because we realised that Tony's success – or the show's success – could be maintained without Sid. He was a marvellous foil, but he could work separately.'

Hancock had already begun to question the motivation behind Sid's character and examine the scripts more closely. Galton and Simpson recall at least three being rejected. Hancock felt there was too much emphasis on Sid's criminal lifestyle. It was not a moral issue, he explained to Main Wilson, it was simply that Sid had played a crook for six years and it was all getting 'too corny'.

Another reason, equally valid in the comedian's mind, for ditching Sid was Hancock's desire to concentrate on films and his hunger for stardom. Hancock had been 'introduced' to cinema-goers in 1954 in *Orders Are Orders*. It was, so far, his single big-screen appearance. Since then, and through-out the six-year run of Hancock's own radio and television shows, Sid had appeared in no less than 40 films. It was *Hancock's Half Hour*, not its leading actor, which had found fame among the ordinary people of Britain. A star, Hancock reasoned, 'is someone who is out of reach'.

It was a philosophy totally at odds with Sid's own. 'The sort of billing I like is, "Billy Bloggs and Sally Brown in . . ." and then underneath, "with Sid James",' he told one feature writer. 'That suits me fine. If I get above the title, they'll get the idea that I'm too pricey, and they'll stop ringing up and saying, "Sid, I've got a little part in my new picture. It's only three or four days, but it's a nice one." I don't want them to stop doing that.'

Not that Sid wouldn't have thought seriously about it if the right role had been offered. Part of the problem was that, to producer and directors, Sid would always be the gravel-voiced fiddler you ultimately forgave. On screen and off, he would remain 'good old Sid'.

'The part I really want is a real mean so-and-so, but no casting director will even put me up for a part if the guy is the slightest bit mean,' he explained. 'Sometimes I think I am going to get a break when I read the script. But by the time I get around to it, the bloke's a nice, kind, lovable old crook all over again.'

The invitation to attend the BBC meeting was vague and noncommittal. Sid left his Gunnersbury Avenue home in high spirits. When he returned he was close to tears. He was more upset than Valerie had ever seen him. 'Tony doesn't want me in the show any more,' he finally explained. 'He wants to go it alone.'

Having delivered his ultimatum at the MacConkeys 'summit', Hancock's cowardice – as ever – stopped him short of confronting his own actions. This 'out of the blue betrayal' as Sid once described it to a close friend, left him shattered. 'What hurt most,' Val adds, 'was that it was the BBC who broke the news and not Tony himself.'

Hancock, it seemed, had discussed his decision with almost everyone but Sid. Years later Liz Fraser, who had appeared in both the radio and television *Half Hour*s, admitted, 'Sid didn't know about this, but Tony told me he was worried that "Hancock and James" were becoming a fixed double-act in the eyes of the public. Tony never had the courage to talk it over with Sid.'

The way in which Sid was eventually given the news – while Hancock rehearsed and recorded as if he had nothing to hide – left Sid 'devastated', claims Fraser. 'There had never been any deterioration in the relationship between Sid and Tony; suddenly it just stopped. Sid was distraught, he just couldn't believe it.'

News of the split between Hancock and the nation's 'number one feed' broke as Sid was on location at Chatham Dockyard. He was making *Watch Your Stern* with Kenneth Connor and Hattie Jacques.

Sid, quite rightly, denied there had been any form of confrontation with Hancock. Years later he admitted he had 'argued with Tony for days – argued like hell' to prevent the break-up. Sid unsuccessfully attempted to persuade Hancock to complete at least one more series together – 'but only one'. Hancock, somewhat dismayed by the publicity his decision was attracting, felt himself backed into a corner. 'I told him he was crazy,' Sid recalls, 'but he had made up his mind.'

For public consumption Sid went along with Hancock's reasoning of needing to try something new and adventurous. 'You can't go on doing the same thing. I don't care who you are or how good you are, the public gets sick of the sight of you.' But the way in which Hancock had planned and executed the parting – as an open secret with Sid in the dark – rankled deeply. Sid admitted he never got over the feeling of hurt. It also brought to an end one of the most prosperous periods in his career. 'We could have made a fortune if we'd stuck together,' he said. 'But Tony had a thing about repetition. It sent him crazy.'

If Hancock was openly frustrated by Sid as a foil, he had shown no sign of wanting to end their friendship. The pair had had just one stand-up row. They were playing pontoon during a break in rehearsals. Sid stuck on twelve. The move infuriated Hancock, who claimed it was illegal. Sid defended himself by saying Hancock had invented the rule because he was losing. What impressed the onlookers was not that the pair were blazing away at each other – itself unique – but the fact that Sid and Hancock had subconsciously slipped into their TV personas and appeared to be acting out yet another Galton and Simpson sketch.

The writers themselves agree the time was right for a change. Alan Simpson still agrees with Hancock's claim that his association with Sid James had turned into a Laurel and Hardy partnership. 'Wherever Tony went in the street people would shout out, "Where's Sid?" '

'Tony's gripe was that he didn't seem able to appear without Sid James,' adds Ray Galton. 'And Sid seemed to be appearing in every film that was being made in Britain. So Tony thought it was time he reasserted his own personality.'

Exactly how many films Sid James had appeared in since his arrival in Britain fourteen years earlier was a mystery. The

figure spirall[...]
ever, kept th[...]
credited ap[...]
Rank was r[...]
claimed Si[...]
months lat[...]
BBC radio[...]
figure was [...]

For the [...]
records he [...]
island sojou[...]
and Hamm[...]
illustrated [...]
do bring b[...]
thing is I g[...]
makes me [...]
music, it doesn[...]
kind of lift out of it.'

Sid was still smarting from the sp[...] last radio series – the sixth – had ended [...] December. Sid's final television appearance with Hancoc[...] was little over a month away. Change, he conceded to the programme's host Roy Plumley, was inevitable. The public was sick of underhand Sid. 'You will notice in the last few Hancocks that we are drifting away from that – it is played out, it is not funny any more.'

To remind him of the 'old times and old laughs and the old team', Sid included an extract from *Sunday Afternoon at Home*, a radio *Half Hour* in which 23 Railway Cuttings is a scene of boredom and inactivity as the occupants attempt to while away a British Sunday.

The final television *Half Hour* was broadcast on 29 April. Sid and Hancock would work together again, but only to re-record old material. In their biography of Tony Hancock, his ex-wife Freddie Hancock and David Nathan wrote of the troubled comedy genius: 'There was a ruthless streak in him which allowed him to cut out of his life all those who had contributed to it but were

.' It was a description
id's attitude to his past
t.

lizabeth Grevler, was kept to
ng remembers talking to her
telephone. When Elizabeth gave
ter, Sid wrote back saying 'enough
gatory Christmas and birthday cards
rprise gift – a photograph of Sid on the
Cowboy. Across the bottom he had
zzy and Gary – love Granpa.' Unknown to
wife, Toots Delmont, had less than a year to
d in agony, crippled with arthritis. Reine, Sid's
as still a resident of the Jewish Old Age Homes in
esburg. Her health was also failing. When she died,
as 'too busy' to attend her funeral.

ack in his native South Africa the Bantu Self Government
Act of 1960 provided for the division of the non-white
population into tribal units, the abolition of their existing
representatives in Parliament, and the creation of self-
governing 'native states'. Apartheid had arrived. Sid, who
had witnessed – and experienced – discrimination at first
hand, was harassed by the Press for a comment. By now he
was a British citizen. His response, although sincere, was
guarded: 'I believe that all men are equal, black or white,' he
said. 'I hate segregation.' The full-blown condemnation of
apartheid was never forthcoming.

The offers were tempting. The BBC, desperate to keep
Sid under contract, hurriedly formulated plans for *The Sid
James Show*. Associated Television wanted to sign him for
Val Parnell's *Merry Go Round*. Sid, after advice from his
agent, had already turned down an approach from Associ-
ated Rediffusion.

Against all his instincts, he was being nudged towards
stardom. Never slow to chance his arm backing a racehorse
or greyhound, Sid was not about to lengthen the odds on his
own career. Freed from the rigid rehearsal schedule of

Above: Sid and Meg with their daughter, Reine. Sid was already having an affair with Valerie Ashton and the marriage was doomed.

Right: Together again: Sid with his daughter, Reine, at a friend's wedding. He had been separated from Reine's mother Meg for two years.

Above: Sid and his third wife Valerie: he was thirty-nine years old and she was fifteen years younger when they married.

Right: Sid with his daughter Susan and son Stephen in the garden of their Gunnersbury Avenue home in Ealing.

Sid was in debt the minute he landed in England in 1946. Money was a theme which dominated his personal life and professional career.

Left: Sid, heavily disguised, plays his first joint lead as Henry Clavering in the 1949 film, *The Man in Black*. Fishing was later to become a passion.

Below: One of Sid's favourite films was *Silent Enemy*, the true story of the wartime adventures of Commander Buster Crabb. Sid played CPO Thorpe.

Bless This House: opening a Wolverhampton housing estate Sid insisted on the location and companion for the publicity shots. (*Express & Star*, Wolverhampton)

Above: Whisky,
cigars, flights, cars –
even crates of
apples. Sid's
publicity deals were
legendary. Whether
it was swapping his
face for a free tape
recorder ...
(© Grundig (GB) Ltd)

Right: ... or a
supply of rum for
his appearance at a
Bournemouth
fishing competition.
(*Daily Echo*,
Bournemouth)

Carry on London: Barbara Windsor had never wanted to appear in the show – Sid persuaded her to join the cast and to become his mistress. (*Express & Star*, Wolverhampton)

The Empire Theatre, Sunderland, where Sid James collapsed and died on stage – and where comedian Les Dawson claimed to have seen Sid's ghost. (*Sunderland Echo*)

Hancock's Half Hour, he would think carefully before he even considered tying himself to a new television show – 'It's got to be good; after the Hancock show it's got to be good.'

In June, Hancock began work on his first solo film, *The Rebel*. Within weeks Sid had signed the contract on a television series of his own. It would be called *Citizen James*. The writers would be Ray Galton and Alan Simpson.

Not even the title was original. It was inspired by the Welles' film *Citizen Kane*. 'The storyline didn't come from anywhere in particular,' admits Simpson. 'It was exactly the way we had been writing up Sid for the Hancock shows. We just took Sid away from Hancock so he could carry on working on get-rich-quick schemes.'

In their outline for the first script Galton and Simpson describe 'Sidney Balmoral James' as 'self-employed, and a man of some forty-something summers and very hard winters. His face bears testimony to a difficult life, careworn, craggy and lined.' They point out, however, that he is not a crook. 'A parasite, public enemy, evil to society, yes . . .'

The writers had been given an office at Elstree studios during the shooting of *The Rebel*. Between rewrites for Hancock they spent an equal period producing material for Sid – although they still disagree on the motive. Alan Simpson believed the split was never a 'bolt from the blue' for Sid James. 'Hancock honestly believed Sid understood the problem,' claims Simpson. 'Hancock was more shocked by the public reaction.'

Galton, however, maintains that Sid was 'terribly upset' by Hancock's decision. 'If we thought Sid knew and understood and wasn't shocked,' Galton asks, 'why did we write a series for him? Because we felt sorry for him. It was purely out of sympathy for being ditched.'

One attempt to reunite Sid and Hancock – albeit for less than a minute – was swiftly vetoed by Hancock. Galton and Simpson suggested a cameo role for Sid in *The Rebel*, in the same way Bing Crosby makes a brief appearance in Bob Hope's solo films made after their *Road* movie partnership ended. The writers wanted Sid to appear as a customs officer towards the end of the film. Hancock rejected the idea as 'old fashioned'.

Citizen James ran for exactly two years and spanned thirty-one episodes. Sid, in a vain attempt to turn over a new leaf, makes a stand for various downtrodden individuals and lost causes only to be bitten in return. On the way he repeatedly relieves Liz Fraser, his long-standing girlfriend, of much of the profits from a drinking club she owns, and manages to inspire hero worship in his sidekick, William 'Bill' Kerr. Duncan Wood – who produced the first series while still producing Hancock's final series for the BBC – had decided that all three leading members of the cast should use their own names.

Citizen James would be the last contract negotiated for Sid by his agent Phyllis Parnell. Their working relationship had become increasingly strained as petty issues surfaced and were left unresolved. One of Parnell's complaints was that Sid's friendship with several radio, television and film producers often led to offers of work being made direct to him at Gunnersbury Avenue. Parnell was only informed when negotiations were complete. Sid did little to heal the wounds. Unknown to his agent, he had formed Arts Management Services a year earlier.

On 14 June 1960, Parnell complained to Bill Cotton junior at BBC Television: 'I am extremely surprised that you approached Sidney James direct regarding *Juke Box Jury*, particularly as we have been handling this artiste for fourteen years, and I thought everybody was aware of the fact.'

News of Parnell's chagrin filtered back to Sid. Within forty-eight hours he had sent a hand-written letter to Eric Maschwitz, head of television light entertainment at the BBC, informing him that his contract with Archie Parnell and Co was due to expire at the end of August and would not be renewed. From 1 September, Sid told Maschwitz, all his

136

'business' would be handled by his own company, Arts Management Services Ltd, based at Gunnersbury Avenue. Fearing Phyllis Parnell may be able to claim commission on any option clauses written into contracts she had negotiated while handling Sid, which might be taken up by the BBC after the end of August, he wrote the next day to Tom Sloan at BBC Television. In exchange for not adding option clauses to contracts currently in the pipeline, Sid offered his 'personal undertaking' to accept any situation comedy the corporation might ask him to do during 1961 for the inclusive fee of £525 per programme.

Sid – and Valerie as head of James (Arts) Ltd – believed they knew enough about the entertainment business to keep any future agent's commission for themselves. By January the following year it was clear they needed help. The first contract signed by Arts Management was for a 17 September guest appearance on *The Billy Cotton Band Show*, for which Sid received 256 guineas. The first episode of *Citizen James* was broadcast on 24 November. And on Christmas Day, Sid appeared in *Christmas Night with the Stars*, recorded at the Riverside Studios. When a letter from Tom Sloan arrived at Gunnersbury Avenue on 4 January 1961, it was obvious Sid had made a grave error by 'freezing' his fee on a second *Citizen James* series.

Sloan was pressing Sid for a decision on a second run of thirteen programmes, possibly between October and December. No mention was made of the fee. One problem was Tony Hancock, to whom the BBC had made a similar offer. Galton and Simpson had written both scripts. If Hancock – who was not prepared to commit himself until the transmission of his spring series – agreed, then Galton and Simpson would obviously be unavailable to write *Citizen James*. 'In the meantime,' Sloan informed Sid, 'we are seriously considering Wolfe and Chesney as your alternative writers . . . We would also like an opportunity of discussing with you possible changes in format, which

137

indeed may become inevitable if Ray and Alan are not the writers.'

Shooting for Sid's second *Carry On* film was originally scheduled to start at Pinewood during November 1960. It was delayed because of the sudden illness of Hattie Jacques. During the intervening two months Norman Hudis trimmed Jacques's part and created a new role for Liz Fraser, a piece of casting which pleased Sid. Fraser was an obvious favourite. The pair were already working together in *Citizen James*.

During the filming of *Carry On Regardless*, Sid knocked himself out after slipping and crashing down a flight of stairs. While the actor was recovering, Thomas and the crew moved on to the next scene. There was no need – or time – for a retake. Sid had delivered his lines at the top of the stairs and his unscripted descent was edited out.

Negotiations were also under way for a new radio series. It was the BBC's second attempt to give Sid his own comedy vehicle. Seven months earlier a trial recording of *The Sid James Show* had been scrapped. Executives considered the script 'poor and un-funny'. This time producer Tom Ronald hired the team of Ronnie Wolfe and Ronald Chesney to write the scripts. The BBC's original title for the series was *What's the Odds*. 'The idea came from above and in many ways we had to do it,' says Wolfe. When he and Chesney were told BBC radio wanted Sid cast as a crooked estate agent they suggested renaming the series *It's a Deal*.

At the end of January 1961, Sid signed a contract with the BBC for a thirteen-part series to be broadcast on the Light Programme. His split with Parnell had obviously not registered with the corporation's drama booking department, who inadvertently sent the contract to Phyllis Parnell at Golden Square. The BBC was still unsure about Sid's ability to carry a radio comedy on his own. In many ways its fears were justified. Sid had shone as Hancock's sidekick. Even his recent appearance on *Educating Archie* had been as a guest. The corporation wanted to play it safe. Established radio series invariably started in the autumn and ran for twenty-six weeks through the winter. The summer was left vacant to try out new writers and ideas. *It's a Deal* was earmarked for a summer airing. In the end the BBC relented, and the first of thirteen programmes went out on 9 March 1961.

The part of Sid's partner went to Dennis Price. The pair had only just finished filming the water-borne comedy *Double Bunk*. Wolfe and Chesney intended to exploit the public image both actors had cast for themselves. The character notes for the first episode read:

SIDNEY JAMES – now in the property game – is the boss of James Investment and Property Undertakings Ltd. The firm, established two or three years, operates from offices in Mayfair – and, thanks to Sid's scheming, is quite prosperous. But Sid is very ambitious – wants to crash into the real big-time international property set – but is hampered by his background, and lack of education. So, like many real-life property tycoons, he has found himself a front man who is . . .

DENNIS PRICE is a Mayfair playboy from a distinguished family – has been expelled from some of the finest schools in the country – but nevertheless, because of his approach and impeccable manners, he is 'accepted' where Sid isn't, and is of great value influencing people and winning friends . . . to suit Sid's business schemes.

Wolfe and Chesney had done more than distil the essence of Sid's stage character. The role they had created for him was ninety per cent Sid.

Although Sid and Dennis are both rogues, they are different in many respects. Sid, dressed in the finest that Cecil Gee can offer, drives a Jag and lives in a flat off the Bayswater Road. Dennis buys his suits in

Savile Row, drives a vintage Bentley and lives in a mews flat. Sid looks after his money. Dennis is wildly extravagant. Their approach to a business problem also differs. Where Sid wants to slip a borough surveyor a handful of fivers to get a shaky scheme passed, Dennis evokes the 'old school tie'.

Sid was now an established comedy actor and busier than ever. The coming year would also see his final straight role in a British-made film, the MGM motor-racing drama *The Green Helmet*. Of the thirty-seven films Sid was yet to make, all but two would be comedies. The exceptions were a lightweight musical and an easily forgotten South African thriller.

With several film offers already in hand, Sid could not spare the time for detailed negotiations. He turned to John Kennedy, a theatrical impresario and agent. Kennedy circulated a letter on 24 February 1961, announcing he was now 'Sidney James's sole agent'.

Wolfe and Chesney had pitched a film idea to Sid. He loved it. The next step was to find an independent backer or sell the comedy to an established production company. The film – *All Abroad* – was never made. A laugh-a-line *Carry On* movie, it was conceptually ahead of its time and could only have been produced under the tight financial management imposed by the *Carry On* partnership of Peter Rogers and Gerald Thomas. 'There was no way we could make it, it would have cost millions,' Wolfe now admits.

The plot-line would certainly have qualified for the Rogers–Thomas series. It is certainly funnier than *Carry On Abroad*, which Sid would make eleven years later. In *All Abroad* Sid is the owner and courier of a small travel company attempting to outwit an equally dodgy rival during a tour of Europe. The writers wanted to shoot the entire film on location. 'It was a good idea that worked well,' admits Wolfe. 'We were simply not experienced enough at film-writing. Sid really wanted to do it, but everyone we approached told us we couldn't take a coachload of actors right across Europe. It was impossible.'

One attempt to raise the necessary cash involved a meeting at Kennedy's Curzon Street office. Wolfe and Chesney arrived to find a beautiful young actress 'arranged carefully on the sofa'. During a break for drinks Sid nudged Wolfe aside. 'Have you got the casting complete for this television thing you're doing?' he asked. Wolfe and Chesney were working on a comedy series set in the dressmaker's workshop of Fenner Fashions. Sid nodded toward the sofa. 'Have you got a part for Judy?'

Later that year Judy Carne spoke the opening words in one of Wolfe and Chesney's longest-running series, *The Rag Trade*.

Another actor, now a television producer, who attended several of the Gunnersbury Avenue parties, will always remember the couple as 'Sid James and Lady Valerie'.

'In many ways that is exactly what they were. Sid was the jester made good, and Valerie was sophisticated and lady-like and always in control,' he says. 'Valerie gave Sid the one thing his talent could not deliver – respectability.'

Sid's own description of his third wife was slightly more down to earth. 'She's attractive, sexy, a wonderful cook and a wonderful mother. She's everything a man could want.'

Sid's attitude to sex was Victorian: it existed, and he enjoyed it. Sex, as Sid once explained to Wolfe, was quite separate from love. He could not understand Wolfe's indignation at his conducting a passionate sexual affair while showing every outward sign of being a devoted family man. 'There was something inside him which failed to understand why it was wrong,' said Wolfe. 'To Sid, having an affair was one thing and being married to Valerie was another. There was something inside him which failed to make the connection.'

Another colleague who found Sid's extramarital excursions difficult to understand was Hattie Jacques. Having worked with Sid on more than forty-five *Hancock's Half Hours* and, so far, one *Carry On*, she had witnessed her

141

co-star's flirtations first hand. 'It got so bad,' Jacques once admitted, 'that I took him aside and gave him a dressing down.' Sid stood there in silence, amazed by the actress's matronly lecture and her prodding finger. When she'd finished, Sid smiled, cupped her face in his hands and planted a wet kiss on her forehead. 'God,' he said, 'you're sexy when you're angry.'

In reality Sid's sexual conscience was walking a tight-rope. The one thing guaranteed to make it wobble was any form of lewd or suggestive behaviour in front of Valerie. On more than one occasion Sid over-compensated. Sid and Val were on holiday in France with Tony Hancock and his wife Cicely. While in Paris, Hancock insisted the quartet visit a certain restaurant. What he hadn't told Sid was that the establishment was more famous for its risqué menu than its culinary prowess.

So far the holiday had been a success. Hancock, always a lover of France, had been generous with his money and hospitality. The four chatted over an aperitif as the waiters fussed around the table – until the bread arrived. Each roll had been fashioned and baked to resemble the male genitals. Sid munched his way through the crusty testicles and oversize penis with obvious unease. Hancock beamed like a mischievous schoolboy.

But the joke wasn't over. Hancock, who claimed to visit the restaurant regularly, insisted on ordering the dessert for Cicely and Val. When the ice cream arrived it, too, was shaped like a giant penis and dripping in thick, white cream. There was only one house rule, announced Hancock. The women were not allowed to use a spoon or fork – they had to lick it with their tongues.

Sid erupted in anger and embarrassment. He stood up and informed Valerie – who was quite willing to join Cicely in entertaining the waiters and other guests – that they were leaving. When she protested, Sid stormed out of the restaurant.

In the light of Sid's rash promise over his fee there was little John Kennedy could do to get the BBC to offer more for the second series of *Citizen James*. Other changes, though, were readily accepted. Galton and Simpson were unavailable. They had begun work on their second classic television comedy, *Steptoe and Son*. The pair would never write for Sid again. Kennedy agreed the new writing team should be Sid Green and Dick Hills, who went on to produce numerous scripts for Morecambe and Wise. Bill Kerr had decided to drop out after the initial six episodes as Sid's henchman. He was replaced by Sidney Tafler. When the idea of a third series was mooted in November 1961, Kennedy began to earn his reputation as a 'tough negotiator'.

Bush Bayley had been given the job of producing the third series of *Citizen James*, scheduled for transmission in the autumn of 1962. Bayley approached John Kennedy to see if Sid would consider yet another series. Preserved in the BBC archives is a single sheet of paper on which Bayley scribbled an *aide-mémoire* of what the BBC had in mind, prior to his telephone conversation: 'Thirteen programmes ... First call July ... Recordings to be decided ... Exclusivity for year ... January–June (no call) ... Offer 650 guineas inclusive.' Kennedy had other ideas. Below are more notes, dated 10 November, and made during his conversation with Sid's agent: 'Kennedy says he's been offered £1,000 by ITV, not inclusive ... He can get £1,000 and even £1,150 for a spectacular ... Won't consider less than 750 guineas.'

It is true that Independent Television was making overtures to Sid, but the figure of £1,000 was Kennedy's opening gambit in the BBC negotiation and bore no relation to what ITV was willing to pay for his client.

While Sid was filming at Pinewood, negotiations continued between Bayley and Kennedy. In November they concluded the terms of a third – and final – series of *Citizen James*, details of which Kennedy listed in a letter from his Curzon Street office the following day. It was the highest fee Sid had ever received for a television series and gave him unique control over certain aspects of production. The first three clauses show just how desperate the BBC were to retain Sid James and the clout Kennedy could wield in his client's favour: '1. Sidney James will undertake to do thirteen half-hour shows for a fee of £750 for each show; 2. It is agreed the script-writers Hills and Green have been commissioned and signed to write the series; 3. Sidney James will have approval of all scripts and the director.'

News of Kennedy's success did little to lift Sid's underlying depression. *Citizen James* appeared popular with the public. Shooting for *Carry On Cruising* was scheduled for early January. But Sid had yet to find the 'spark of magic' in the *Carry On* films he relished in *Hancock's Half Hour*. In many ways he felt guilty at not being there to protect his friend. Sid was missing Tony Hancock more than he would have imagined or admitted. There was also growing pressure from the public for a reunion. The BBC was still receiving a stream of letters from angry and frustrated fans. 'What Sid and Tony had together was something unique and the public loved them,' said Valerie James. 'They clamoured for them to get back together.' Around the house Sid talked of little else, she recalls. 'He never wanted to be a star on his own. He was content to share the limelight.'

Tony and Cicely Hancock were on holiday in the South of France. Valerie, having persuaded her husband to confront Hancock head on, wanted the matter resolved as quickly as possible. Sid agreed they should fly to France immediately.

When they arrived Hancock appeared overjoyed. He was tanned and relaxed and eager to talk about new projects. Hancock had completed his final series for the BBC earlier that year. Shooting for his second film, *The Punch and Judy Man*, was not due to start for several months. Late one night, after Cicely and Valerie had gone to bed, Sid suggested it was time the two men should work together once again.

To Sid's surprise Hancock readily agreed. Knowing how

much Hancock's consumption of alcohol affected his judgement – and memory – Sid waited for the morning. This time Hancock brought the subject up. He wondered about a new series or possibly a show. 'We came away very happy,' adds Valerie. 'Tony, for all he had said in the past, was equally keen on them starting again.'

Two weeks later a short, hand-written note arrived at Gunnersbury Avenue. It was from Hancock. He had changed his mind. He did not want to restart the partnership. And that, he rebuked Sid, 'is my final word on the subject'.

CHAPTER NINE

On Saturday, 4 November 1961, Sid and Valerie drove the fifteen miles from Ealing to attend a barbecue and fireworks party at the Wraysbury home of Sid's agent, John Kennedy. By the end of the evening Sid was in hospital – and being hailed a hero.

John Kennedy was renowned for his extravagant and expensive parties. Among the sixty film and theatre stars who arrived at his riverside country cottage near Windsor were two of his clients – Sid James and Tommy Steele – and a heavily pregnant Diana Dors.

A little after 10 p.m. Kennedy was forced to put an end to a drunken round of skylarking in the garden. Fireworks were being thrown. Dors, expecting her second child, moved to the safety of the living room. Although they only met briefly, Sid had worked with Dors six years earlier on the film *A Kid for Two Farthings*. Her husband, actor Richard Dawson, was not at the party. She began chatting to Sid and Valerie.

'It was a very pleasant party, but there was a bit of larking,' Sid recalled. 'Val was a bit worried and Kennedy told someone who was throwing jumping crackers about to stop being a fool. Whoever it was was a right lunatic.'

Suddenly there was a blinding flash followed by a succession of ear-splitting explosions. A wicker basket, in which the fireworks had been stored, had ignited. Guests dived for cover as rockets and roman candles ricocheted off the ceilings and walls.

Valerie screamed at her husband: 'Look after Diana – she's pregnant.' The front porchway was engulfed in flames. Almost every curtain and item of furniture on the

146

ground floor had been set alight by the exploding fireworks. There was only one way out, through the kitchen.

Valerie and Kennedy crawled on all fours. Sid shielded the near-hysterical Dors as best he could. Once in the tiny kitchen they smashed the windows. Valerie clambered to safety and then helped her husband with the pregnant actress. As he was about to follow, Sid caught sight of another female guest attempting to reach the kitchen. He dragged her to the window and pushed her through, gashing his finger on the broken glass.

Outside the scene looked like a battlefield. Guests stood about in shocked silence. Others attended the injured. Ambulances later took seven burn victims to hospital. There was a cluster of men and women attempting to resuscitate a showbusiness solicitor who suffered a heart attack only seconds after escaping uninjured from the fire. He later died. From inside the burning cottage Sid could hear the screams of trapped guests. He ran around the building trying to find a way in. Each time the flames beat him back. Firemen later found the charred body of one of Kennedy's male friends.

Sid was taken to a Slough hospital to have his cut finger dressed and stitched. The next morning newspapers around the world carried the story of the tragedy. All praised 'hero Sid James'.

Sid's relationship with Kennedy never recovered from the trauma of the Guy Fawkes tragedy. Although he was about to conclude the hard-fought deal for the third, and final, *Citizen James* series, Kennedy was less successful with other attempts to cash in on Sid's ever-increasing popularity. In February 1962, he wrote to John Davidson, assistant head of light entertainment at Broadcasting House, enquiring whether the BBC would be interested in a radio series based on *Citizen James*. Hills and Green had already agreed to write the script. The idea was turned down. Scribbled across the corner of Kennedy's letter is an unsigned comment: 'There would be no market for this series.'

Others were more eager to exploit his popular image. The

147

1962 Summer Exhibition at the Royal Academy in London included a portrait of Sid by Ruskin Spear.

Sid's first film appearance as himself came in *We Joined the Navy*. Sid put in a special guest appearance. Perhaps the producer and director hoped that drafting Sid into the story of a carefree naval commander and three cadets who get themselves entangled in the affairs of a small Mediterranean country would salvage an otherwise desperate farce. The film sank without trace – unlike Sid's only other film of the year.

In *Carry On Cruising* Sid plays Captain Wellington Crowther, a veteran cruise captain attempting to cope with the antics of new crew members and amorous passengers. Perhaps the most notable feature of the film is that it was the first of the series to be shot in colour.

Two newcomers joined the cast for *Cruising*. Charles Hawtrey was replaced by Lance Percival after the first of many disagreements about billing, and Dilys Laye was recruited at three days' notice to replace a sick Joan Sims.

Laye, who went on to star in three more films in the series, found Sid 'one of the most unselfish actors' she had ever worked with. 'He was a professional who never lost his cool. No matter how bad the conditions he never made anyone feel inferior.' They quickly became friends – a situation, Laye felt, frowned upon by Sid's wife.

Laye met Valerie only once. She and Sid were shooting a lightweight love scene in which she chases him, as Captain Crowther, around the deck of the SS *Happy Wanderer*. Watching stony-faced from behind the camera was Val. 'I don't think she approved,' comments Laye.

Laye's diminutive size made her a natural for the obligatory *Carry On* nice-but-naughty female. But her on-screen temerity belittled her off-screen determination. She quickly became 'one of the lads' with Sid and the technicians. Yet, as Laye recalls, 'Sid never stopped treating me like a lady. He was a gentle man as well as being a gentleman. Sid always made you feel like a woman. His quiet way of talking to you somehow made you feel attractive and beautiful.'

It was a view shared by most of Sid's other female co-stars. Joan Sims once said, 'Sid had feelings of protection about women which some found old-fashioned in the 60s. But I know I appreciated them.' And his old friend Hattie Jacques – who once warned him about his numerous affairs – described Sid as generous and helpful to most people, 'especially women'.

Sid's chivalry entered Pinewood legend after one incident on the *Carry On* set. Peter Rogers had treated three or four Members of Parliament to lunch at the studios. The cast and crew were warned to be on their best behaviour during an afternoon tour of the sound stage. It soon became obvious, however, that one of the visitors had had far too much to drink over lunch. Sidling up to one of the prettiest young actresses the MP began making loud and equally lewd suggestions. The set fell silent, frozen by the man's political clout and personal ineptitude – until Sid came to the young woman's rescue. 'Here, that's enough of that,' he said. 'Just cut that out.'

Carry On Cruising was Sid's third film for director Gerald Thomas. Excluding TV specials, Sid would return to Pinewood and the *Carry On* set every year for the next twelve years. It was enough to make him the undisputed male star of the entire series. Other regulars may have clocked up more appearances – Kenneth Williams (25 of the 29 films); Joan Sims (24); Charles Hawtrey (23) – but Sid and Barbara Windsor always had a physical presence which perfectly suited the characters they were asked to portray.

Various attempts have been made to justify the apparently everlasting appeal of the films – what Kenneth Eastaugh describes in *The Carry On Book* as 'an incorrigible phenomenon'. In the late 1950s and early 60s, when seaside holidays were still popular and Britain still shared a holiday camp sense of humour, the early films breathed life into this fat-lady–thin-man postcard fun, the origin of which George Orwell knew as a place where 'marriage is a dirty joke or comic disaster, where the newly-weds make fools of themselves on the hideous beds of seaside lodging houses, and the drunken red-nosed husbands roll home at four in the morning to meet the linen-clad wives who wait for them behind the front door, poker in hand . . .'

Sid's sexual prudery was strangely at odds with a career relying more and more on innuendo and flagrant *double entendres*. For a man who found it hard to control his high-sparking libido, Sid found it impossible to cope with any form of impropriety. On more than one occasion he would publicly step in to defend a young woman's honour while, a short time later and in private, he would shamelessly attempt to seduce her.

It was during the filming of the musical *Three Hats for Lisa* that Sid's appetite for sex was put to the test. In the film Sid plays a London cabby recruited by a foreign film star to help steal three typically English hats. One actress cornered the director Sidney Hayers. 'I have been here four weeks and no love,' she protested. 'No man has made love to me.' It was not long before she decided Sid was the man to put things right.

One afternoon, between takes, Sid was informed that the actress wanted to see him. Knocking on her dressing-room door he was asked to wait. Three or four minutes later Sid was invited in. She was waiting open-armed – and stark naked.

When it came to understanding his own sex appeal, Sid was an innocent. 'Women were crazy about Sid,' explained fellow *Carry On* star Jack Douglas. 'He used to pooh-pooh the idea, but Sid was undoubtedly a sex symbol.'

Just as Sid had spent the previous year 'afloat' in the Mediterranean, he was now destined to spend 1963 behind the wheel of a taxi. Had it not been for a decision by Rank executives during editing, Sid's only film that year would never have been added to the *Carry On* stable. As it turned out, *Carry On Cabby* is one of the best. Not originally intended as a *Carry On*, the film was shot in black and white. *Call Me a Cab* was based on an idea by Sid Green and Dick

Hills, who had written the second and third series of *Citizen James*. To develop the plot Peter Rogers hired Talbot Rothwell. He would write the next nineteen films in the series. To the *Carry On* regulars, Gerald Thomas added Jim Dale and Amanda Barrie. Kenneth Williams was absent for the first time since *Sergeant*.

Rothwell's arrival as the *Carry On* scriptwriter – to replace Norman Hudis – heralded a dramatic change in the way the British public perceived Sid. To the majority of his fans Sid was still a wideboy, a little older and little wiser perhaps, but still basically the rogue who had deflated Hancock's dreams. Norman Hudis's scripts had already become increasingly ribald, but Rothwell abandoned all subtlety, broadening the concept and delighting in a peculiarly British bawdiness. It suited Sid and his image. It also suited Rothwell. The other stars stepped in and out of roles as the script demanded. To Rothwell, Sid would remain the lecherous, scheming chancer.

The ubiquitous Ted Willis, creator of *Dixon of Dock Green*, was well aware of the potential of cabbies and their custom of providing storylines. In *Taxi* he had created a television series which veered between drama and comedy. In it, Sid is cast as a sourer version of his traditional persona, using his expressive face to reflect on the unfairness of life more than the eye-widening grin of the suddenly spotted opportunity.

Willis sold the idea of *Taxi* to the BBC as a season of twelve 'stand-alone plays'. Each programme lasted fifty minutes, longer than anything Sid had previously attempted for television. The series – broadcast during July and August 1963 – was not a success; the ratings were poor. Partly, the BBC assured Sid's agent, 'because of the decision to transmit during the holiday period'.

By the time Sid had agreed to the second series of *Taxi* he had changed his agent.

* * *

The telephone rang at the London offices of the Bernard Delfont Agency. The call, from Sid James, was put through to the managing director's office. Delfont – later Lord Delfont – was in the middle of a meeting with fellow agent Michael Sullivan. Delfont was not about to ignore a call from one of the country's leading comedy actors.

Sid came straight to the point. He informed Delfont that he wanted to end his association with Kennedy. Could Delfont, Sid asked, recommend a new agent. Delfont cupped his hand over the mouthpiece. 'How do you fancy handling Sid James?' he asked Sullivan. His reply was emphatic: 'Not 'arf.' Returning to Sid, Delfont assured him: 'I've got the very man for you.'

Michael Sullivan was a small, wiry man who had clawed his way to the top of showbusiness management. Distantly related to Arthur Sullivan, one half of the Gilbert and Sullivan partnership, he was the illegitimate son of the P & O shipping magnate, Frederick Allen. By 1964, he was a director at the Bernard Delfont Agency and already handled two of Sid's *Carry On* co-stars, Kenneth Connor and Charles Hawtrey.

Sullivan arranged to meet Sid at his Ealing home that night. He arrived at the Gunnersbury Avenue house to find the family in the final stages of moving out. The house had already been sold.

In the spring of 1961, Sid and Valerie had bought a ten-acre plot near the village of Iver in Buckinghamshire. The land, through which ran the River Colne, backed on to The Coppins, the Duke of Kent's country house. Although they could afford the land, the couple were forced to remain at Gunnersbury Avenue for another three years. An old building on the site was demolished while Sid and Val designed the home of their dreams – 'a six-bedroomed job with a flat for staff'.

Before they moved to Iver in August, the Jameses lived first in 42 Malvern Court in Knightsbridge, and then, from the beginning of April, in 31 Compayne Gardens, close to West Hampstead railway station.

The two men met for the first time. 'There was an immediate rapport between us,' remembers Sullivan. 'We simply clicked.' For Valerie, her first meeting with Sullivan was possibly the high-spot of their twelve-year association. Their working relationship – she as head of James (Arts) Ltd – hovered a degree or two above freezing point. Sullivan tolerated what he felt was Val's over-meticulous attention to detail for the sake of his client and his twenty per cent commission.

Sid began by producing a set of plans for his new home at Iver. The Jameses had already decided to call it Delavel Park. Sullivan studied the drawings. At the risk of going down in showbusiness legend as the first agent to lose a new client after just six hours, he feigned approval. 'It looked terrible,' Sullivan later admitted. 'Even when it was built it had no style whatsoever. It looked like a prison.' Victor Spinetti, with whom Sid would later work, placed it in an architectural niche of its own – 'Golders Green crematorium'.

'This is my dream home,' Sid confidently told his new agent, 'and you are the man who is going to get me the money to pay for it – and by the way I owe the Inland Revenue £35,000.'

Sid's 'confession' to owing the tax man £35,000 appears to have been no more than a crude attempt to manipulate his new agent and fire him with an unfounded sense of urgency. It is inconceivable that under Val's by now legendary management, James (Arts) Ltd should have been allowed to accrue such losses. Sullivan claims he was ignorant of any such deception.

Within forty-eight hours he would come face-to-face with another example of Sid's cunning. On 24 February, Sullivan informed the BBC that the Bernard Delfont Agency was now the 'exclusive agents for Sydney James (*sic*)'. The following day Sullivan answered the telephone at his Regent Street Office. It was an agitated Sid demanding that his new agent come to the Shepherd's Bush studio where he was recording *Taxi*.

When Sullivan arrived, a seemingly panic-stricken Sid explained he needed £600 to clear his gambling debts and buy off two psychotic collectors. Sullivan, who had so far not earned a single penny in commission from the latest addition to the client list, raced back to his West End office and rifled the petty cash box. He topped up the amount from his own wallet and arrived back at the studio to be told by the receptionist: 'Mr Sullivan, there are two gentleman to see you.'

As the two Neanderthals rose Sullivan shoved the cash into their hands. 'It's all there,' he said. 'Six hundred, OK?'

For a moment there was a puzzled silence. Then one of the men said: 'No chum, you're wrong.'

Sullivan's stomach collapsed in on itself. 'What?'

'It's five hundred. That's all we've come for.'

Back in the dressing room Sid ignored his agent's protests over the miscalculation. 'That's nice,' he told Sullivan. 'I could do with that.' As Sid took the £100 the penny finally dropped. 'Like a clap of thunder the truth hit me,' Sullivan later confessed. 'Sid had known all along just how much he owed his bookie. He had simply added an extra £100 to the amount so he would have enough for another bet.'

Sid enacted the same trick on all his friends in turn. Some refused to be taken in a second time. Others simply accepted it as the price of his friendship.

But Sid was not finished with Michael Sullivan. Having lied about the desperate state of his finances and conned his new agent out of £100, Sid was determined Sullivan was not going to turn a profit until he had earned it. Sullivan's letter to the BBC was followed four days later by one from Sid, informing the corporation that fees for the current series of *Taxi* – and any others owing – should be sent direct to James (Arts) Ltd and not to his new agent.

Throughout their twelve-year association Sid James and Michael Sullivan never had a written contract. It was a practice Sullivan insisted on with every client. A single handshake on the first night they met was all that bound them. 'In law you can always break an agreement,' explains Sullivan. 'It is far harder to break someone's trust.'

Sullivan was a wheeler-dealer agent of considerable talent and candour. He once described himself as a 'self-confessed bastard'. But even Sid James could teach him a few new tricks. Between them they became a formidable team.

'The public saw and accepted Sid as a carefree, spend-thrift character scheming to get hold of some quick and easy money to spend on a fruitless chase after romance,' Sullivan said. 'As much as I loved and respected Sid as a human being, he made Scrooge look like a public benefactor.'

In the months that followed Michael Sullivan quickly discovered there were more frustrating problems in hand-ling Sid James. Almost eight years after the formation of James (Arts) Ltd, Val was still taking her directorial responsibilities seriously. For the first time in his career Sullivan found himself answering not only to his client – but also to the client's wife. Contracts were vetted word for word; expense accounts queried. Sullivan found his well-ordered and pleasurable life punctuated by a series of what he dismissed as 'petty telephone calls'. It kindled a smouldering and unresolved animosity between Valerie and Sullivan.

Only Sid's innate deviousness – and Sullivan's lying – defused an otherwise doomed triangle.

There were two parts to every Sid James film contract: the fee that Sid – and ultimately Valerie – accepted, plus a cash top-up negotiated by Sullivan and handed direct to his client. This Sid called his 'back pocket money'. Such was the agent's long-standing chumminess with producers that Sullivan could be relied upon to come up with some kind of arrangement, no matter how big or reputable the film company. Even for the *Carry On*s James (Arts) Ltd was paid just £3,500 for the actor's services. The remaining £1,500 Sullivan delivered personally.

The deception did not stop there. Sid continued to exploit a betting system he had first employed to fool his colleagues during the Hancock days. Between rehearsals or filming for *Hancock's Half Hour*, Sid would often be seen in the corner of the studio muttering into a telephone behind a cupped hand. Passers-by would hear him laying 'a shilling each-way double' or 'two shillings on the nose'. For the suspicious he would later comment, 'Guess what? My tenpenny bet came up. I won five shillings.' Nobody was fooled.

At home in the 1960s, and in front of Val, he employed the same method. Watching the racing on the television Sid would telephone his bets to a primed and conspiratorial bookie. The code was simple. For 'shilling', read £100. An innocent 'five-shilling each-way' invariably plunged Sid another £1,000 into debt.

Whenever Val became suspicious, Sid moved his operation to the home of a friend or fellow actor. Victor Spinetti, who starred with Sid in the comedy series *Two in Clover*, still recalls the early Saturday morning telephone calls. 'Sid would ring to remind me we were rehearsing that afternoon, as if I knew all about it. It was obviously for Val's benefit.'

The same afternoon Sid would arrive at Spinetti's home with his favourite racing paper and a supply of cigars. Never a gambling man, Spinetti found Sid's adrenalin rush contagious. 'I could feel the excitement of it,' he recalls, 'the sheer joy he got from it.'

Sid always regarded the deception over his stake money as 'cheating but basically honest'. As his need for cash grew more urgent, Sid thought up several ingenious ways of skimming extra money from James (Arts) Ltd. One scam he slid past his wife was getting a dresser or make-up artist he was employing to submit an inflated account. Val innocently authorised payment and Sid received a cash rebate.

But very rarely did Sid end the week in the black. Few of his friends recall him celebrating a winner. One exception was the pop star Joe Brown. He was offered a part in the 1965 musical *Three Hats for Lisa*, and still claims he only accepted the part because it gave him the chance of working with Sid James.

All went well until Brown was spotted by the film's

director, Sidney Hayers, slipping Sid a £10 note. The singer was warned of Sid's 'problem', and duly promised not to finance any more of his co-star's investments. 'I never saw the £10 again,' Brown remembers.

A few weeks later Sid tried to borrow another £10. Brown, this time attempting to use amateur psychology to cure Sid of his scrounging, asked Sid to place a second £5 bet. 'I figured that if he lost my fiver as well he would never have the nerve to ask for any more money,' he said. About ten days later Sid cornered Brown to hand over his £125 winnings. 'But he never told me how much he had made on the bet,' admits Brown.

Carry On Spying was the ninth in the series of Peter Rogers–Gerald Thomas comedies. When shooting began on 3 February 1964, it was the second successive production without Sid James.

One new face on the Pinewood set was Barbara Windsor. Cast as Daphne Honeybutt – codename Brown Cow – Windsor was hired to replace Liz Fraser as the *Carry On*s' obligatory busty blonde. She became an immediate favourite with the fans. Despite making only eight more films in the series, Windsor, more than any other actress, is regarded as *the* female icon of the *Carry On* comedies.

Born Barbara-Ann Deeks, Windsor was discovered at the age of thirteen by talent scout Brian Mickey. Another of Mickey's successes was a comedy duo called Morecambe and Wise. After a season in pantomime, Windsor was accepted by a Golders Green drama school where she sat next to Shirley Eaton.

In 1959, Windsor joined the cast of Frank Norman's play about Soho streetlife, *Fings Ain't Wot They Used To Be*. The production's leading roles were taken by Miriam Karlin and James Booth. When *Fings* moved to the Garrick Theatre in February the following year, the audience included veteran BBC producer Dennis Main Wilson. He had already signed Karlin for a new television comedy series entitled *The Rag Trade*. Main Wilson predicted Windsor would never make it as a comedienne because she was 'far too pretty'. It didn't stop him inviting her to join the television cast.

Windsor had been having a long-running affair with a London gangland heavy by the name of Ronnie Knight. Windsor and Knight decided to marry on 2 March 1964. *Carry On Spying* was almost complete.

It would be three more years before Windsor was invited back to Pinewood by director Gerald Thomas. In less than three months, however, she experienced her first encounter with a fellow *Carry On* actor who would change her life forever.

For its 1964 charity gala the Variety Club hired Battersea Pleasure Gardens, originally built for the Festival of Britain thirteen years earlier, and invited more than two hundred celebrities to sign autographs and meet the press. When a photographer asked Windsor to pose with a 'craggy-faced' actor on a boating lake pedalo she eagerly agreed. As the pair drifted away from the shore the man put his arm around Windsor and shuffled suggestively closer.

'I do think you're lovely,' Sid James said, with a lecherous chuckle.

Michael Sullivan sat back in his chair at the Bernard Delfont Agency office and unfolded the telegram.

The block letter message was printed on the thin tele-type strips and pasted across the standard GPO form. Above the message were the words South African Film Studios, Johannesburg. In the terse sentences demanded of telegrams, the sender enquired whether Sidney James would be interested in accepting a role in a South African film. The telegram was signed 'Tokoloshe'. Sullivan did not bother consulting Sid. He cabled 'Mr Tokoloshe' in Johannesburg for more details.

When nothing arrived, Sullivan put through a telephone call to the SAF Studio. 'I want to speak to Mr Tokoloshe,' Sullivan demanded. There was the faint sound of a suppressed giggle. Sullivan repeated his request. 'Which particular one?' the switchboard operator wanted to know.

'We have so many here.' Tokoloshe, Sullivan was politely informed, was South African slang for scoundrel.

Sullivan was eventually put through to Peter Prowse, who explained how he had persuaded the SAF Studios and a syndicate of Johannesburg financiers to back his latest project. The cartel was unanimous in wanting Sid to play the lead.

Among those waiting to greet Sid as he stepped off the plane at Johannesburg's Jan Smuts Airport during the first week of June 1964, were a group of assegai- and knobkerry-waving Zulu dancers – and an eight-year-old boy.

Saul Pelle, from the Meadowlands, had been chosen as Sid's co-star in his first South African film, *Tokoloshe, the Evil Spirit*. The airport authorities had refused to allow publicity staff to bring another of the film's 'actors' – an ox – on to the runway.

In 1946 Sid had left the Union an unknown actor with an empty wallet and bags of ambition. He returned, eighteen years later, a comedy star. Ironically it had taken another South African to realise Sid's potential as a serious actor.

Peter Prowse, a second cousin of the actress Juliet Prowse, had persuaded Sid to take on the character role of a near-blind recluse. The hard-bitten ex-seaman befriends a piccanin who is running away from his kraal because the chief wants to sacrifice him to appease the rain gods. Sid, however, had already decided it was time he returned to South Africa. He had also wanted to show Val his homeland. When the script had arrived at Delavel Park neither Prowse nor Michael Sullivan needed to apply much pressure.

What Sid hadn't bargained for was an unexpected – and uninvited – reminder of his life in pre-war South Africa. Night shooting for Friday, 12 June had been scheduled for an area near the railway footbridge at the top of Johannesburg's End Street. The lights had been erected and the set dressed. When Sid finally arrived more than an hour late he apologised to Prowse: 'We had to stop and help pull a car out of a ditch.'

During a break in the shooting Sid was informed someone was waiting to see him. The man, whom Sid did not recognise, was standing patiently among the jumble of vehicles and equipment. It was another hour before Sid learned that 30-year-old Benny Grevler had flown from Bulawayo to Johannesburg to meet his father-in-law for the first time. Grevler had made the journey from his home in Rhodesia in a bid to reunite his wife with her father. Elizabeth had not seen Sid since her visit to England ten years earlier. Even the news that Sid was a grandfather again failed to persuade him. 'Unfortunately it just cannot be done,' Sid informed Grevler. 'I am just too busy.'

Before they parted Grevler gave his father-in-law a note of the family's telephone number in Bulawayo. Sid never called. But if he was guarded about re-establishing contact with his first family he was not so reserved with old friends.

The telephone rang at Jack Berry's Johannesburg hair-dressing salon. When he answered it Berry was surprised to hear the voice of his former employer. Sid invited his old friend on to the *Tokoloshe* set. Berry wasn't taking any chances; he knew Sid would never change. On his way to the Lonehill Studios, he bought a bottle of gin and some Rose's lime juice, Sid's pre-war favourite tipple. Sure enough, as Berry entered Sid's dressing room he was asked: 'Did you bring anything to drink?'

After five weeks of filming at the Lone Hill Studios outside Johannesburg, Sid's enthusiasm for the part had not diminished. 'This is one of best roles I've ever played,' he said.

Working to a tight shooting schedule and under severe financial pressure, Sid had enjoyed Prowse's firm control. 'Many more famous directors ask the cast how they think the scene should be played, and then we play them that way,' explained Sid. 'Prowse knew exactly what he wanted and we did it that way.'

Not everything submitted so readily to Prowse's demands. The gremlins struck as Sid, dressed in a pyjama top and paper hat, was attempting to film a short scene with

160

fellow actor Siegfried Mynhardt. Sid invites him into his ramshackle home to answer questions on the presence of his young guest. As the hydraulic lift on which the camera was mounted ruined yet another take with a fearsome graunching sound Sid, still in character, turned to Mynhardt and said: 'There's a bleeding chair. You better take the bleeding thing, 'cause it looks like we'll be here for weeks.' It took nine takes before Prowse was happy.

Unruffled, Sid was impressed enough with the studios and the South African film industry to consider returning. 'I would like to make at least two films a year here,' he said, and admitted he was already negotiating for 'something big' that coming November. The 'something big' centred on a script by Bob O'Keefe. It told the 'magnificent story' of South Africa's ex-arch criminal, Willem Goosen. The deal – which would have cast Sid in the lead role – never materialised.

Despite his superstitions, Sid was back at Jan Smuts Airport on Friday, 13 July. Shooting for *Carry On Cleo* was due to start at Pinewood seven days later. It would be another seven years before *Tokoloshe* was released in Britain.

Sid clung to the memories of his friendship with Hancock. Since Hancock's second, and more brutal, rejection their paths rarely crossed. Holidays and social meetings had ended. The final disillusionment came in 1965.

Sid had postponed his holiday in Majorca for a week to return to the recording studio with Hancock. They were to record two *Half Hour* episodes for release on disc. 'It was not a happy experience,' Alan Freeman, the producer, has always maintained. 'By then Tony's sense of timing had gone awry.' Ray Galton and Alan Simpson were also present. Each script had originally been written to run exactly twenty-eight minutes, perfect for one side of a long-playing record. Both sessions were a 'disaster'. Hancock stretched *The Reunion Party* to forty-two minutes. *The Missing Page* was little better at thirty-eight minutes.

Simpson recalls: 'Tony's timing was bad; he was slow; he had no emotion . . . it was dreadful.' It took Freeman and the two writers almost a day to edit out all the pauses and sew the performance together.

The experience was enough for Sid. He swore never to work with Hancock again. Soon afterwards Hancock began to pester Kenneth Williams into joining his stage show. When Williams informed the *Carry On* cast, he claimed Sid replied: 'You'd be mad to work with him again – the man is a megalomaniac.'

In 1965 – eight years after Susan's birth – Valerie discovered she was pregnant for a third time. Sid was fifty-two and delighted. But it was soon evident that things were not going well. When Val's and the baby's lives were threatened she was admitted to hospital. Sid was at home looking after his son and daughter when the hospital telephoned to say Valerie had miscarried. Sid broke down and wept. 'It was the only time I saw Dad cry,' Susan said after his death.

When Sid arrived to visit his wife he was beaming broadly and cracking jokes. As he closed the door on Valerie's private room the smile faded. In the lobby he had been recognised by Ringo Starr. 'Hello, Sid mate,' said Starr. 'Become a daddy again?' The Beatles' drummer was visiting his wife Maureen after the birth of their first child. Sid explained about the miscarriage and was shocked to see Starr's eyes fill with tears. Next day the Beatle arrived unannounced to see Valerie. 'I was crying when he came to my room and he tried so very hard to cheer me up,' she recalls.

Of the two films Sid made during 1965, one remained his favourite of the nineteen *Carry On*s, in which he appeared. *Carry On Cowboy* demanded far more from Sid as an actor than simply the delivery of funny lines. It is, perhaps, the 'straightest' of all the comedies. As always Sid wanted to give his best. During filming Gerald Thomas caught Sid

162

behind the scenery practising drawing and firing his six-shooters. 'He was a little boy in a world of cowboys and Indians,' Thomas said. 'But he took it very seriously.'

When it came to managing his clients' careers, Michael Sullivan had a strategy. Each year was meticulously planned in advance. In Sid's case it invariably entailed a January meeting at Delavel Park. 'I would tell him this year you are doing this, this and this – and I think you ought to try this,' says Sullivan. 'From 1964 I masterminded his career.'

Only twice did Sid refuse or baulk at Sullivan's advice. Both times it concerned fringe benefits of the kind most dear to Sid's heart.

Each year Sullivan inched his client's career forward. Sid had always refused to consider pantomime. Sullivan persuaded him otherwise. As ever, Sid was reluctant to turn down any film offer. Sullivan was more choosy and began negotiating higher and higher fees. It was now time, Sullivan announced, for Sid to make his name in America.

When Sullivan told Sid he was on the verge of signing a deal with Walt Disney in Hollywood Sid backed away. 'I told him he could make millions in America,' recalls the agent. 'He didn't want to know.' The reason, Sid finally admitted, was that without Sullivan in America to negotiate his contracts, his under-the-table payments from producers would have to stop.

A second 'fringe benefit' helped placate Sid, after an uncharacteristic tussle over billing threatened to sink a West End show.

Sid agreed to appear in *Solid Gold Cadillac* with Margaret Rutherford, but only if he received first billing. Rutherford and the producers stood their ground. When they offered equal billing – with both stars' names appearing side-by-side on all publicity material – Sid still refused. For some obscure reason, which Sullivan never discovered, his client demanded to have his name above Rutherford's. The production was about to be abandoned until Sullivan informed Sid: ' "There is a lovely little blonde in the

company and you are going to give her one every night" –
which he did.'

Sid was to make only two films during 1966. The first was
a low-budget comedy called *Where the Bullets Fly* in which a
secret agent saves a nuclear power unit from the Russians.
Sid played a nameless mortician. The second was a *Carry
On* production in all but name. *Don't Lose Your Head* was
not accepted into the *Carry On* series for more than two
years. After the completion of *Carry On Screaming* in the
spring of 1966, Peter Rogers decided it was time to cut his
long-standing ties with Anglo Amalgamated Films, which
had backed and distributed the majority of the *Carry On*
series. The disagreement stemmed from the pressure
applied by Anglo Amalgamated executives that Rogers
reverse his decision to drop Charles Hawtrey from *Screaming* in favour of Sydney Bromley. To appease the
financiers, and publicly to deny press outrage at Hawtrey's
absence, Rogers agreed to reinstate the veteran.

Capitalising on the rift, Rank swiftly stepped in and
offered to take over the winning formula – if not the name.
While happy with the series and its cadre of actors, Rank did
not want to be associated with a title made famous by a rival.
It agreed to the making of *Don't Lose Your Head* – and the
subsequent *Follow that Camel* – as long as the words *Carry
On* were omitted from the title.

Sid appeared in only one of the disputed films, as Sir
Rodney Ffing – pronounced 'Effing' – in *Don't Lose Your
Head*, a Scarlet Pimpernel take-off. Shooting began on 12
September 1966 at Pinewood. It was during the filming that
Sid's tolerance of Kenneth Williams began to wear thin.

Since his arrival in England Sid had confined his work to
a rigid discipline. While in a radio or sound studio, he was
an actor who gave one hundred per cent of his attention to
acting. It was a professional attitude which contrasted
dramatically – and often harshly – with Kenneth Williams's
'jolly jape' mentality. To Sid, acting, even in *Carry On*s, was
something you did and went home, it wasn't something you
tried to enjoy.

When speaking feed lines off-camera to an actor in-shot, Williams invariably pulled funny faces in an effort to make them laugh or throw their concentration. Sid reacted angrily to such antics. 'Cut that out,' he'd snap at Williams, 'I'm trying to do a scene.'

'The trouble with Kenny is that he's just like a little schoolboy,' explained fellow *Carry On* actor Peter Butterworth. 'He does something and he knows he's gone too far, but he just doesn't know how to say sorry.'

Another James 'hate' was appearing in drag. Not because he thought himself unfunny in a woman's clothes, more because he felt it belittled the macho image he had taken such trouble to develop. When a drag scene in *Don't Lose Your Head* combined with Williams's asides the result was explosive. The script demanded that Sir Rodney – alias the Black Fingernail – dress as a giggling girl while being questioned by Williams as Citizen Camembert, chief of the secret police. As Sid appeared on set in a wig and dress Williams purred, 'Ooh, I couldn't half fancy you!' The camera crew joined in with wolf whistles and equally suggestive invitations. 'Shut up the lot of you,' snapped Sid as he stomped on to the set. 'Let's get this scene shot and out of the way.'

Whatever Sid thought of his fellow actors was usually confined to the privacy of his Iver home or, after a particularly trying day, over a drink with his agent Michael Sullivan. Kenneth Williams returned to his London flat and meticulously recorded his vitriolic judgement on his fellow cast members. It was not until Williams's death in 1988, and the subsequent publication of his hand-written diaries, that the extent of his loathing for Sid James came to light.

Williams viewed his own role in *Don't Lose Your Head* – as he did the series itself – as 'liberally sprinkled with filth'. Viewing the completed film the following year, he recorded in his peculiarly effeminate style: 'Sid James really does look terribly battered and old. Very unattractive when he's making love to the girls in it – all rather disgusting.' In December 1973 he saw the film again. Once again Sid warranted a second swipe: 'One forgets if one is away from the face for long enough, but it is so bashed and creviced that it gets in the way of any articulation, and oh dear! he is such a bad actor – he reveals his embarrassment at every line. Each utterance is done in the "I have got to get rid of this" sort of fashion and the embarrassment is passed straight on to the viewer.'

A professional snob, Williams desperately needed to maintain an emotional distance between himself and the non-acting members of the *Carry On* crew and the general public. Although Sid was too much of a gentleman to allow his fans to irritate him in public, he enjoyed being considered 'one of the boys' by the technicians, an attitude which annoyed Williams intensely and, in his own mind at least, posed Sid as a threat to his self-image as the true star of the *Carry On* series.

Peter Rogers remained adamant that the on-set rivalry should not spill over into the public arena. 'We always said no one is going above the title. The title is the star of the series,' repeated Rogers. 'For that reason there was no single *Carry On* star.' It did not stop him or his director-partner taking action to protect those stars the public considered favourites – and would pay to see – and dealing ruthlessly with the egos of others. Charles Hawtrey, who had appeared in all five previous films, was dropped from *Cruising* after a wrangle over a silver star on his dressing room door and bigger billing. 'It was a difficult situation,' admitted Thomas. 'But with the best will in the world we just could not bill him above Sid James.'

Sid, however, was not averse to sowing his own mischievous seeds of discontent – especially if he could raise Kenneth Williams's blood pressure a notch or two.

After the conclusion of *Carry On Teacher*, but before Sid's arrival, the cast had been offered a profit-sharing scheme. Every single agent rejected the offer, plumping instead for higher fees. The idea was mooted again in the mid-60s. 'I decided that to keep down budget levels it would be an idea if the artists formed a kind of repertory and took a percentage of the films' profits,' Peter Rogers admitted in the *Mail on Sunday* thirty-five years later. 'But their agents said "no". If they had taken percentages the artists would be very wealthy today and would still be getting cheques through the post.'

One agent who denies he was ever asked to consider any kind of percentage deal was Michael Sullivan. 'People think that, with the compilations and endless television screenings of the *Carry On* films, Sid should have been rich,' explains Sullivan. 'They hired him for seven or eight weeks' work and that was it: no profit share, no repeat fees, no TV payments.'

With salaries up for grabs after each subsequent film, Sid enjoyed prodding his fellow actors with exaggerated claims of his financial worth. There is no doubt Sid James and Kenneth Williams were the two highest-paid members of the *Carry On* cast. Sullivan claims he could never squeeze more than £5,000 out of the producers. Hattie Jacques and Barbara Windsor got exactly half that. For Joan Sims, it was a rate that never changed in the nineteen years between *Nurse* and *Emmannuelle*.

The profit and loss account for each *Carry On* film – like the shooting schedule – was meticulously worked out. *Carry On Sergeant* cost £74,000 to make. By the sixth film in the series, *Carry On Cruising*, production costs had doubled. By 1970, the final bill for *Carry On Henry* topped £223,000. Every film in the series turned a profit. Most were in the black within a month of release and, for the majority of the films, most backers saw a 400 per cent return on their investment.

Cruising also marked a new deal for Rogers and Thomas. In addition to their £20,000 fee, the pair divided their share of the profits on a fifty-fifty basis. But while the quiet, dog-loving Rogers might spend his profits on porcelain or other collectables, his younger partner had far more in common with Sid. Both had served in the Middle East during the war, Sid with the South African Entertainment Unit and Thomas as an officer with the Royal Sussex

Regiment. Thomas, like his actor friend, was a self-confessed 'gregarious-optimist', and both enjoyed good living and good company, travel and show-business functions – particularly when the food and drink were being added to someone else's account. They soon became close personal friends.

'He was a great family man who loved children,' recalled Thomas shortly before his own death in 1993. With the Jameses' move to Iver, Thomas became a regular visitor. And when Sid and Valerie accepted dinner invitations to the director's own home Sid would invariably irritate Thomas by playing with the children or telling bedtime stories while the meal cooled and spoiled downstairs.

The first time Thomas became aware of 'Sid the hoofer' was when Sid took over the role of Nathan Detroit in *Guys and Dolls*. Thomas had witnessed 'Sid the character actor' two years earlier when he had edited *The Venetian Bird*, a film in which Sid plays a dubious undertaker with an even more suspect Italian accent.

Thomas, always a schedule-driven director, increasingly came to rely on Sid during the making of the *Carry On* series. When a film is shot to a high-speed, no-frills script it is useful to have a 'one take' actor like Sid in the cast.

For Thomas, his friend's great ability lay in producing a laugh from the most unpromising situation. 'Sid was never a comedian, never a stand-up comic,' admitted Thomas. 'He was no good without a script. Ask him to open a fête and he was lost. But his interpretation of a script was superb. We never wrote funny lines for Sid. His comedy came out of the situation and his interpretation of other people's funny lines. He was a remarkable actor with impeccable timing.'

Always a respecter of the script and its creators, Sid seldom demanded changes. On the rare occasions when he suggested adding or cutting a line, the film invariably benefited. Thomas kept a tight rein on his fine-tuned sense of humour. He may have laughed at the spontaneous comic suggestions from the cast, but he seldom allowed them to clutter the script or, more importantly, slow down the day's shooting. Only one of Sid's jokes is known to have reached the screen. Shooting for *Don't Lose Your Head* started at Pinewood on 12 September 1966. During one scene Charles Hawtrey, as the Duc de Pommfrit, is awaiting execution on the guillotine. Sid's suggestion was for someone to rush up with a message and for Pommfrit to say, 'Drop it in the basket, I'll read it later.'

But some of Sid's funniest responses were never seen by his fans. Dreaming up situations to catch Sid out became a regular pastime for the *Carry On* technicians. During one film Sid has to walk into shot and pick up a suitcase. Unknown to Sid the floorcrew had loaded the empty case with weights. It took two of them to lift it back into position. The cameras rolled, Sid's efforts to move the case became even more hilarious, and the entire crew collapsed in laughter.

Timing the production of each *Carry On* film was also critical to its financial success, a situation which Sid's agent, Michael Sullivan, exploited to the full. Most films in the series were made in the spring or autumn, when the stars were free from winter pantomimes and summer seaside shows – when Rogers would have had to pay more to engage them. During the free months of July and August 1966, Sullivan booked Sid to play at the Pier Theatre, Bournemouth. Throughout the Christmas holiday and into the New Year he starred in *Robinson Crusoe* at the Golders Green Empire. His co-star was fellow *Carry On* actor and friend Kenneth Connor.

Between the two bookings Sid agreed to clash swords with the indomitable Peggy Mount and her Force Ten voice. *George and the Dragon* was the creation of Vince Powell and Harry Driver. The first episode – broadcast on 19 November 1966 – shows Mount as Mrs Gabrielle Dragon securing employment as housekeeper to Colonel Maynard, played by John Le Mesurier. The only challenge to her authority is Sid as George Russell, the colonel's chauffeur. The resultant conflict proved so popular it lasted for twenty episodes and spanned three years. The secret of the show's success lay in the exploitation of the two very different personae that both Sid and Peggy Mount had established for themselves.

In real life Mount was far from the bossy battle-axe she invariably portrayed. But she had realised early on which way her career was heading when she read the stage directions of her first theatre success, *Sailor Beware*. It said: 'Enter huge, noisy, overbearing wife.' A character equally suited to her was Mother Ada in the Cockney family classic *The Larkins*, and later in *Lollipop Loves Mr Mole*.

Mount – who Sid once admitted in many ways reminded him of his mother – had worked with her new co-star only once. They appeared in the mid-1950s adaptation of the Brian Rix farce, *Dry Rot*. Mount had never met John Le Mesurier before.

As the first episode of *George and the Dragon* was being filmed Mount realised how 'unselfish and generous' an actor Sid was. She tells the story: 'I had stood right in front of his camera. Sid didn't say, "Oh, come on" – he simply knew that I was an idiot and didn't know any better. He didn't get cross. He just moved me round and we went on with the scene.'

The series – combining Mount's bluster, Sid's conniving and Le Mesurier's cool charm – was an instant success. When, early in 1967, rehearsals started for the second series, Mount soon realised which of the trio Thames Television listened to most.

Each episode was rehearsed and shot back-to-back. The cast had expected a weekend off. Late on Friday it was announced all three stars would be on call for weekend publicity events. 'It's just not fair,' Mount protested. She was obviously upset.

Sid calmly sat Mount down and told her to have a cup of tea. When he came back a few minutes later Sid announced, 'It's cancelled. Go home. I've cancelled it.'

On 13 May 1967 – less than a week after his fifty-fourth birthday – Sid was at Thames Television's Borehamwood studios filming *George and the Dragon*. The cast had been working hard for weeks. All seven programmes of the second series had been rehearsed and recorded in quick succession.

During the morning Peggy Mount noticed Sid was slightly out of breath. In his dressing room and in private he complained to Valerie about a pain in his chest. At lunchtime Michael Sullivan arrived at the studio and took his client for a drink. Sid complained of indigestion. Valerie was taking no chances. She telephoned the family doctor and described her husband's symptoms. When she told Sid the doctor wanted him to go to hospital for an immediate cardiograph, he refused. Sid was adamant: 'after we've recorded the show'. Valerie promised not to say anything.

'It was hard going,' recalls Valerie. 'Through the afternoon the pain got worse and was really taking a hold.' After the recording the couple raced home. Sid drove so fast he was stopped by the police. 'Hello, Sid,' said the officer as he squatted beside the driver's door. 'You were over the speed limit you know.' Sid was pale and shaking. He spoke softly. 'Please bear with me. I'm in the middle of a heart attack. I've got to get home as quickly as I can.' The officer looked at Sid, and then Val, and waved them on.

Valerie James and Michael Sullivan have both told in print different stories of what happened next. Both claim their version of events is correct.

According to Valerie, Sullivan played no part in the episode. 'Early the next morning a specialist came and Sid agreed to a cardiograph,' claims Valerie. 'It confirmed our fears. The specialist told me it was very serious and that Sid should go into hospital immediately.' At first Sid refused. The doctor insisted.

Sid got out of bed slowly and painfully, putting on a towelling dressing gown. Then he walked downstairs and out through the front door to the waiting car. 'Just before he got in he turned to look at our home. He looked for a long moment with tears in his eyes,' said Valerie. 'I stood beside him. I knew what he was thinking. "Will I ever see this place again?" '

Sullivan was by now living at Denham, only a short drive from Iver, and Delavel Park. In his autobiography, *There's No People Like Show People*, he claims Sid's heart attack was sudden and devastating.

At two-thirty the next morning Sullivan says he was woken by the telephone. It was Valerie. He could hear the panic rising in her voice. 'Mike, for God's sake come over. Sid's had a heart attack.'

When the agent arrived, a coat flung over his night clothes, a doctor was already at the house. Sid was in his pyjamas and lying unconscious on the living-room couch. A wrangling over ambulance boundaries was wasting vital seconds. The doctor was demanding that Sid be taken direct to a specialist hospital twenty-seven miles away at King's Cross in central London. The local ambulance control refused. Despite Sid's deteriorating condition it claimed only a London Ambulance service vehicle could make the run.

The doctor took Sullivan aside. 'There just isn't time,' he told the agent. 'Do you think you could drive him to hospital? I'll go ahead in my car and arrange everything, but you must keep your speed below twenty-five miles an hour.'

Sid was carried to Sullivan's large and spacious Austin Van Den Plas and wrapped in blankets on the car's rear seat. It was, Sullivan freely admits, the 'longest and most nerve-racking' journey of his life. He listened constantly to Sid's laboured breathing. Val was cradling her husband's head. Each time the car went over a bump on the road Sullivan feared he might have killed his friend and client.

When the news broke on the Saturday afternoon a spokesman for the Royal Free Hospital would say nothing more than that the *Carry On* star had been admitted 'for a rest'. Sid spent the next three weeks in an oxygen tent. When he was eventually allowed home he spent three months recovering in a downstairs room and promised his doctors he would stay away from the stairs.

The bitterness between Valerie and Sullivan is fuelled by claims by Sullivan that for days the doctors would only allow Sid's agent into his hospital room. His wife was confined to the corridor outside.

'I was the only visitor he had in fourteen days,' Sullivan claims. 'I held his hand. Sid kept saying, "Where's Val? I want Val." But they wouldn't let her in.' Eventually, when the crisis was over, Valerie was told she could be with her husband. 'I felt so sorry for her,' adds Sullivan. 'I was upset and sorry for the way the doctors kept her out.'

When the telephone rang at Delavel Park Valerie instantly recognised the slow, deep, familiar voice. 'How is he then?' There was no conventional greeting. No 'hello'. No preamble.

'Oh, Tony.' Valerie was almost crying with delight. It was a long time since she had heard from Hancock. 'Sid will be so pleased to know you phoned.'

The call was short. Hancock listened and then wished his old friend well. The conversation ended as abruptly as it had begun. It would be the last time the Jameses would hear from Tony Hancock.

CHAPTER TEN

By October 1967 – less than five months after the heart attack had almost killed him – Sid James was back at work.

Peggy Mount was eager to restart the delayed second series of *George and the Dragon*. She was not sure Sid would survive the rigours of a live recording session. Mount is convinced 'there was only one reason why Sid came back so early – money'.

'He was an absolute monster with his money,' said Mount, who admits to lending Sid the odd £20 to put on a horse. 'He was a gambler, he had several mortgages on his house and his children were in private school. He hadn't saved a penny. It was either work or go under.'

Sid rejoined Peggy Mount and John Le Mesurier at the Borehamwood studios for rehearsals. The director, Shaun O'Riordan, had warned the entire cast not to allow Sid to overexert himself. When he was not on his feet acting, Sid was ordered to sit. A chair was placed in the wings for the live recording of the first episode.

The audience welcomed Sid back with cheers and loud applause. Waiting to make her entrance, Mount could see Sid was obviously enjoying himself. In his excitement Sid burst into an unscripted dance. The audience roared with approval. Sid responded with a second, more vigorous jig. Suddenly he clutched his chest and fell into the wings and out of camera view.

Mount remembers: 'Sid was gasping for breath. He looked dreadful. I honestly thought he was going to die.' As Sid sat panting in a chair the recording was halted. Valerie, watching from the control room, knew nothing about her husband's collapse. The audience was told the zip on Peggy Mount's dress had broken and they would have to wait until it was mended. The studio rippled with laughter. Sid insisted on finishing the episode and the series.

Within days he also returned to the *Carry On* set. His long-time friend Gerald Thomas was anxious to have Sid back on the film's list of credits. The actor's worsening heart condition – together with pressure from distributors Rank for greater international appeal – had already cost him the lead in *Carry On Follow That Camel*. The role of Sergeant Nocker was taken over by *Bilko* star Phil Silvers. This time, though, Thomas wasn't taking any chances – Sid spent most of the filming of *Carry On Doctor* in bed as a patient.

Late in 1967 Sid was driving down London's Piccadilly. It was one of his first outings since his heart attack. The taxis and buses slowed to a crawl as a dishevelled figure lurched across the road and finally took refuge on a traffic island. As Sid passed, the unshaven face and sleepless, sunken eyes turned to examine him. There was no flicker of recognition. It was Tony Hancock.

'He looked dreadful, quite dreadful,' remembered Sid. 'He really looked so miserable. I tried to pull up and get over to him. I got the car parked, but by then he had disappeared. He was so full of liquor he didn't see me. I wish to God I had been able to catch him, because little things like that can change people's lives.'

It was the last time Sid ever saw Tony Hancock. On 24 June the following year Hancock's body was discovered in his Sydney apartment. He had committed suicide. His troubled life was summed up by Spike Milligan, who wrote: 'One by one he shut the door on all the people he knew, then he shut the door on himself.'

Michael Sullivan had secured a second summer season for Sid, this time at Torquay's Pavilion Theatre with John Inman. He was to return in 1971 for another season.

The late winter of 1968 was spent filming a new television series. *Two in Clover* was an early, less subtle version of *The Good Life*. It was a cross between the American series *Green Acres* (city dwellers move to country) and *The Odd Couple* (ill-matched pair share apartment). The Welsh actor Victor

175

Spinetti, who had never previously worked with Sid, had recently finished a stage version of *The Odd Couple* when he was approached by Thames Television about the new series. The production also reunited script-writers Vince Powell and Harry Driver, producer Alan Tarrant and Sid James – all of whom had worked on the highly successful *George and the Dragon*.

The first series of seven episodes was broadcast between 18 February and 1 April 1969. It was followed, almost a year later, by a run of six more.

Sid spent his fifty-sixth birthday at the Kruger Park. It was the first birthday he had spent in South Africa for 23 years. The visit, like the *Tokoloshe* trip five years earlier, had been prompted by an invitation to take part in a film. This time he had agreed to a part in an oddball comedy adapted from a Cora Swemmer book by Howard Rennie. It was originally called *Don't Shoot the Shareholders*. Within days of Sid's arrival (but not because of it) the film was renamed *Stop Exchange*. It was never released in Britain.

Sid had been hooked by the way-out script, which he felt was in line with the lunatic humour surfacing at the time in England. His shooting schedule was also mercifully short – restricted to just one-and-a-half days. The next two days he spent relaxing with Valerie in the Kruger Park before flying back to London.

His belief in the South African film industry remained firm, despite an incident four years earlier in 1965, when Sid had criticised the South African authorities for not exploiting the potential of *Tokoloshe*.

The film – which did not get a British release until 1971 – had failed to get a showing at the 1965 Cannes International Film Festival because someone had not been 'on the ball' enough to submit a judging print on time.

'It's always a good thing for a young country to have its work judged by international standards,' Sid had said. 'Particularly as South Africa is aiming to build a film industry on a vast scale.' The climate was the industry's biggest asset but, felt Sid, the country desperately lacked expertise.

Those who saw Sid for the first time since his 1964 stay were shocked by the change in his appearance. He was still the jaunty showman smoking big cigars, but his heart attack had taken its toll on his health and his attitude to work. Sid, with Valerie's insistence, had slimmed down both his waist and his workload. His carefully controlled diet included just one main meal a day. A pipe – and the occasional cigar – had replaced the chain-smoked cigarettes, and alcohol was restricted to two or three drinks each evening.

'I've given up trying to work in the theatre all night and on the sound stage all day and smoking cigarettes in the car on the journeys between, the way I used to,' he admitted. 'I was living on my nerves.'

Although looking thinner and feeling healthier than he had done for some years, Sid's schedule was as demanding as ever. Traditionally all new Sam Cree comedies opened for a summer season in Blackpool's Grand Theatre. His latest one, *Wedding Fever*, was no exception. Sid had already contracted to do a second series of *Two in Clover*. To accommodate one of its stars, Thames Television agreed to film the series locally. Each morning Sid would arrive at the television studio, and twice each afternoon and evening he would energetically throw himself around the stage.

When Spinetti called at Sid's dressing room he was shocked at the sparse surroundings. Faced with a three-month run most performers would attempt to transform what little space they have into a home-from-home. Sid didn't believe in wasting money. To take a telephone call he had to climb two flights of stairs. To make a cup of tea he went down a flight to the wardrobe department. There was very little furniture. Sid even refused the free help of a dresser. The man's £30 wages would have been paid by the theatre management – but Sid was not prepared to part with the £5 weekly tip.

'It was as if he didn't want to spend the money on making the dressing room comfortable,' recalls Spinetti. 'He was all alone with no one to get him out of his wet clothes or protect him from visitors. He wanted that money to put on another horse.'

One Monday morning Spinetti arrived at the studio and casually mentioned a weird dream he had had the week before. It concerned a horse and he thought Sid might be interested. Spinetti described watching a galloping horse. Clutching its neck and trapped by the reins was a young woman. From somewhere – he didn't know exactly where – Spinetti became aware of the phrase 'Sun God'.

Sid exploded. 'You fucking bastard, why didn't you tell me sooner?' Spinetti watched as Sid frantically began flipping through a copy of *Sporting Life*. 'You could have been given thousands, you bastard.' Sid waved the results of Saturday's Newmarket racing under Spinetti's nose. Running in the first race had been a horse called Entangled Maid. The second race was won by Ra, another name for the Sun God. The prices were 33–1 and 5–1. Sid had missed the chance of a 165–1 double.

One piece of advice Sid repeatedly offered Spinetti – and most of his other co-stars – was to invest in diamonds. Wary of the tax man, Sid salted away uncut diamonds for his retirement. He showed them, only once, to Michael Sullivan. 'These were not peas,' Sullivan recalls. 'These were stones worth a small fortune.'

The Blackpool run of *Wedding Fever* was followed by a sixteen-week tour that ended in Great Yarmouth one Saturday night in September 1970. The entire cast was then driven through the night to Heathrow Airport in time to catch a plane for South Africa.

On 23 September, Sid – and the entire cast of the London production of *Wedding Fever* – opened at Johannesburg's Civic Theatre. It was his first appearance on a South African stage since 1946. Other members of the cast of the successful farce included Sandra Hale, Maureen Norman, Dorothy Dampier, Beryl Mason, John Inman, Pat Kean, Nicholas Brent and Bill Tasker.

Sid had won the hearts of both the Civic Theatre

management and its audiences – and now they wanted to make his impression permanent. On 3 October 1970 – the final day of *Wedding Fever*'s two-week run – Sid was invited to take off his shoes and socks and step into a tray of wet cement. He was the thirtieth visiting star to leave a concrete impression at the theatre.

The play then transferred to Cape Town. The day after it closed Sid caught a flight to England. Within forty-eight hours he was back at Pinewood for the shooting of *Carry On Henry*, the twenty-first in the series.

The film's original subtitle was *Anna of a Thousand Lays*. It was changed, after shooting was complete, to *Mind My Chopper*. The final publicity slogan, beneath a picture of Sid James, was *A Great Guy with His Chopper*. It was a classic *Carry On* double entendre which meant more to Sid than any other member of the cast realised – least of all Barbara Windsor.

Sid and Windsor had worked together on four previous *Carry On* films. They had waved at each other across the muddy field in which much of *Carry On Camping* is set, but *Henry* was the first time the pair had played opposite each other. To Windsor – who had first seen Sid on stage in *Guys and Dolls* – his talent was undiminished. One scene included a lively dance called a garotte. Director Gerald Thomas wanted the scene shot in one take as the pair chatted. Sid – whose costume as Henry VIII was the one previously worn by Richard Burton in *Anne of a Thousand Days* – learned the steps with apparent ease.

For Sid, the film was the start of an obsessive infatuation and his most disastrous affair.

Michael Sullivan can recall the moment – only days into the shooting schedule – that his client announced: 'I don't know what happened but I have decided to make love to Barbara Windsor.' He later confessed that he had fallen for his co-star from the first moment he'd 'clapped eyes on her'.

The fact that Barbara Windsor should eventually replace Liz Fraser – with whom Sid was infatuated in the early 1960s – was hardly a surprise. For Sid it wasn't so much sexual chemistry as sexual fantasy. Both were *Carry On* leading ladies. And both portrayed slim-waisted, top-heavy blondes – Sid's lifelong preference.

Despite their encounter on a Battersea boating lake, Sid James and Barbara Windsor had only worked together on two films prior to their first *Carry On* – *Carry On Doctor* in 1967. They never met on set. In 1954 they both appeared in the classic comedy, *The Belles of St Trinian's*. And Windsor makes a brief appearance as a telephonist in *Make Mine a Million*, in which Sid stars with Arthur Askey.

Sid's first hint at seduction was crude and uncharacteristic. One morning, while shooting *Carry On Henry*, Sid handed Windsor a passionfruit. She had never seen one before. 'This is nice, Sid,' Windsor said innocently. 'What do I do with it?'

'Sid took great delight in slowly peeling it,' recalls Windsor, 'and then showing me how to eat it. To put it mildly, his performance was highly sexual, strictly X-rated stuff.' Windsor laughed off the incident.

A few days later Peter Rogers innocently invited Sid and Windsor to join him for lunch at the Mirabelle, a swish and expensive Mayfair restaurant, to discuss a Christmas TV spin-off, *Carry On Long John Silver*. The *hors d'oeuvres* were delivered and Sid lowered his voice. 'You know something,' he informed Windsor, 'they're not as big as they look on screen.'

'What aren't?' asked the actress.

'Your bosoms.'

Windsor's 'dizzy doziness' was fuelling Sid's fascination: her outrageous wardrobe; the way she changed her hairstyle almost every day; her sharp tongue; the way she wiggled when she walked. For Sid it was simple lust, but it would soon turn to a deep and damaging love.

In one *Henry* scene Windsor steps naked into a bath. As ever, the director Gerald Thomas called for a closed set with only essential crew members present. Somehow Terry Scott, another actor whose libido fell only fractionally short of Sid's, managed to hide himself among the off-set shadows.

Suddenly Sid's voice boomed through the pre-shot silence. 'Hey, Terry,' he said, grabbing the startled actor and marching him off the set, 'I'm not going to tell you again – come away!'

No one had the nerve to do the same to Sid James. 'Bloody people,' he mumbled. 'They've only got to hear you're going to show your bum and they're like bees round a honeypot.'

In 1971 *TV Times* announced the arrival of a new television family – the Abbotts. The magazine described the family – created by comedy writers Vince Powell and Harry Driver – as 'just another group of people who find themselves – unfortunately, they think – related and, at the same time, divided by that ever-present generation gap'.

The character that Powell and Driver created to head their fictional family was not far removed from Sid himself. During his working hours, Sid Abbott was employed as a representative for a stationery firm. Off duty, his interests in life were alphabetical – ale, birds and Chelsea Football Club.

Sid's long-suffering wife, Jean, was played throughout the comedy's five-year run by Diana Coupland. Leeds-born Coupland had a show-business history almost as long as Sid's. At fourteen she had been a £2-a-week singer with a popular 1940s dance band. By the 50s she was being regularly booked by some of the era's most popular big band leaders, including Geraldo, Stanley Black and Cyril Stapleton. Although the series, *Bless This House*, made Coupland a household name it also changed her life. When the series ended in 1976 with Sid's death, she found it so difficult to shed her 'Jean Abbott' image that she was forced to abandon television work and turn, instead, to the stage.

Sid and Jean's two misunderstood and bolshie teenage offspring were played by Robin Stewart and Sally Geeson, whose sister Judy would play opposite Sid in two future *Carry On* films.

Vince Powell and Harry Driver had worked with Sid on his two previous Thames Television series. 'He was a comedy writer's dream,' admits Powell. 'Because if a line was not all that brilliant he would have that dirty laugh at the end, and everyone would laugh – and he had the knack of turning ordinary lines into brilliant lines.'

Even a studio ban on alcohol did not deter Sid. Trouble with inebriated actors had forced Thames to bar all drinks from dressing rooms. To outwit the director Sid bought a large bottle of mouthwash. The whisky-coloured liquid was replaced with Cutty Sark. For weeks the two writers would pop in to Sid's dressing room for a 'mouthwash'.

Sid's ploy came to an abrupt end one day after a dress rehearsal. The show's director had followed Sid back to his dressing room to discuss a difficult line. 'I've got a terrible throat,' he suddenly announced. 'You don't mind if I have a mouthful of gargle?'

The task of producing the series was given to William G. Stewart. It was Stewart's first experience of working with Sid and his own personal brand of professionalism. Watching the first day's rehearsal, Stewart had nagging doubts. The script – and Sid's interpretation of it – wasn't working. It wasn't funny.

Stewart took his star aside. 'You don't seem to have any energy,' he told Sid. 'We've got to do something.'

'That's not the way I work,' replied Sid. 'I don't want to leave my best fight in the gym.'

Stewart remained unconvinced. But when the show was recorded Sid delivered one of the funniest performances the producer had ever seen. For the next six years Stewart never saw Sid's full performance until the cast reached the studio. 'He knew exactly what he was doing,' admits Stewart. 'Every one of those odd grimaces and looks to one side and boyish little whimpers – he knew what they meant and how to use them. Sid was a very clever actor and a very clever sod.'

Clever enough indeed to enlist Stewart's help to conceal his gambling from Valerie. Stewart – like Sid's bookmaker – was taken in by the mock secrecy. The Jameses had gone to the South of France for a week's holiday. During the last day's shooting for *Bless This House*, Sid had handed Stewart a bundle of fivers and asked him to pay his betting account while he was away. When Stewart arrived at the book-maker's he was met with a conspiracy of silence. 'The man behind the counter looked dumb and tried to tell me I was in the wrong shop. He insisted, "Sid James doesn't owe us any money." '

Stewart, convinced Sid had given him the correct address, demanded to see the manager. He, too, denied any knowledge of the actor's gambling debts. 'In the end I slammed the money on the counter and said I was going to leave.' As Stewart was about to walk out of the door the manager called him back. 'OK,' the man said. 'But don't tell anyone. Sid's not supposed to gamble.'

The producer has his own theory on why so many people willingly protected Sid. 'He didn't need protection, he was just a nice man,' explains Stewart. 'Some people have that quality. They attract niceness in other people. You just couldn't help but like Sid James.'

Powell and Driver's motive in *Bless This House* was to exploit the friction they claimed exists in most average families. As *TV Times* put it: 'The Abbott family live in a state of perpetual turmoil, varying between hysterical neutrality, punctuated with occasional moments of veiled hostility, and open warfare.' Regardless of the accuracy of their statement, by the end of its first series *Bless This House* was an established hit, attracting almost nine million viewers each week, and ending 1971 as the fifth most popular programme.

The Abbott household was also a hit with younger fans. For the second time in his career Sid found himself the co-star of a cartoon strip. Exactly ten years after his *Film Fun* adventures with Tony Hancock ended, Sid was back – this time in a *Bless This House* strip.

Writers and directors had long since realised that any part which did not reflect the public's image of Sid would not be accepted. Sid played Sid. The dividing line between his private and public personae had progressively faded. Sid, both on and off screen, remained basically Sid. He slipped in and out of roles as easily as one of his exclusive Cyril Castle suits. Each contract stipulated that his stage suits should be made-to-measure and Sid's to keep.

'Nobody could ever think of me as a star,' he confided. 'I'm just a jobber. People can either take me or leave me. All I can do is play myself.' But that didn't stop Sid exploiting the parallel lives that the writers had created for him.

During the Hancock years he couldn't walk through Covent Garden or any of the other London markets without the porters shouting at him, 'What fiddle are you on today, Sid boy?' And when television audiences adopted him as the public-spirited Citizen James, he would frequently be approached by earnest men and women eager to enlist his aid in good causes. Sid enjoyed every minute of it, particularly when members of the Press – who should have known better – were sucked in by his crinkle-faced honesty. On this level they were never lies, never devious, rather they were personal jokes created by Galton and Simpson, echoed by Sid, and solidified as fact by the media. One *Radio Times* interview, published in 1962, reported that 'he was christened Sidney Balmoral ("and that's a dead liberty, for a start!") James'. Thirty years later the myth was still around, this time proffered by *Movies* magazine, which also should have known better.

The truth lay even nearer the surface than Sid realised. The image may have been nothing more than a bit of fun, but when Talbot Rothwell typed the story outline for the first of an annual series of Thames Television *Carry On Christmas* specials, the echo – if not the original sound – was strangely in tune with Sid's own philosophy. The first page of the outline read: 'Everyone knows that Scrooge was a mean old B——, but not even Dickens could have anticipated what happened when Ebenezer kept Dr Frank N. Stein and Dracular short of development money; and refused to lend Robert Browning the fare to take Elizabeth Barrett to Venice; and evicted Cinderella from her basement kitchen for being behind with the rent.'

The first *Carry On Christmas* was transmitted on 24 December 1969, starring Sid as Scrooge and six of the *Carry On* regulars. Frankie Howerd made a guest appearance as

Robert Browning. It attracted the highest viewing figures of any programme during Christmas week.

Predictably, the following year saw the production of *Carry On Again Christmas*, with Sid hopping as Long John Silver and Barbara Windsor as busty cabin-boy Jim Hawkins. Two more followed in 1972 and 1973 but, with the use of judicious repeats, Thames Television was able to sell the ITV network a programme every year until 1975. Sid appeared in only one more special, first broadcast in 1973. 'This year Sidney James is working as Father Christmas in the fairy grotto of a department store,' explained Rothwell in his outline. 'He looks back nostalgically as he imagines what Christmas must have been like in the stone age era; in Sherwood Forest with Robin Hood and his Merrie Men; in an eighteenth-century drawing room; and in the trenches during the First World War.'

On 21 September 1972, Sid landed in Australia for the first time. Greeting him at Sydney's Mascot Airport was a gaggle of eager journalists – and a public health officer. Sid had not been warned that anyone setting foot on Australian soil requires a smallpox vaccination. Sid was duly quarantined and inoculated.

The oversight provided good copy for the waiting reporters. For those who wanted more details, Sid saw nothing wrong with lying about his past. His arrival, he enthusiastically explained, was a 'homecoming'. His connections with the Antipodes were, it seemed, numerous. One newspaper reported: 'His father and mother were playing in Fuller's Circus in Sydney the year before he was born. And so he got his name.'

Another claimed: 'His father was Australian, which technically makes him one of us.' Although Sid did admit that he 'didn't know exactly where in Australia' his father came from.

Even his motive for coming to Australia was only a half-truth. Sid was due to open at the Comedy Theatre in Melbourne on the last day of September. The play was a new farce by Sam Cree entitled *The Mating Season*. 'You can't just do television and films all the time,' Sid explained. 'It reaches the point where people turn on, see your face and make rude noises. But to do plays you must really love the business.'

In reality, Sid loathed touring. As ever he needed the money, and Australia, Michael Sullivan had persuaded him, was a country willing to pay for a new face. In Britain Sid had advertised everything from apples to holidays – all came with free samples. While in Melbourne Sid, as Robin Hood, had agreed to film a series of cigar commercials – another favourite product. Sid was not averse to screwing money from anyone, even total strangers.

Sid and Valerie flew on to Melbourne. Awaiting them were the inevitable journalists and photographers. As Sid entered the room set aside by the airport authority for interviews, he was greeted by a young radio reporter. Sid was obviously not in the best of moods. Graham Guy introduced himself and asked if Sid would answer a few questions for the listeners of station 3XY in Melbourne. As Guy was about to switch on his tape recorder he noticed Sid was glaring at him with fixed eyes. 'Pay me the money,' Sid demanded.

'Sorry?' said Guy, taken aback by the obvious aggression in Sid's voice.

'If you want to talk to me, pay me the money first,' insisted Sid.

Unsure of whether he was the victim of a James joke, Guy fumbled to switch on the recorder and continue the interview. With no fee forthcoming, Sid's irritation increased. The interview lasted less than five minutes. Each question was met with a dry, monotone voice and a single-sentence answer. Sid tried the same ploy with every journalist in the room.

Sid's obsession with Barbara Windsor was taking hold, and he took his infatuation with him. One of the two television specials Sid had contracted to compile in Australia was called *Carry On Sid*. The half-hour solo comedy features Sid in a television control room presenting a series of clips from a variety of *Carry On* movies. Sid demanded that they include sequences from *Carry On Camping, Abroad* and *Henry*. All featured Barbara Windsor wearing the minimum amount of clothes. When the TV station, HSV7 Melbourne, failed to provide the saucy clips, Sid demanded they be sent direct from the *Carry On* production office at Pinewood.

Sid then fashioned a script with himself as a lecherous 'bird fancier' who never quite gets the girl, who always happens to be Barbara Windsor. Two sequences feature Windsor naked in a shower and about to enter a bath. Sid repeatedly misses the scene either by failing to watch the correct monitor or by being distracted by a ringing telephone. As the clips progress Sid masters the slow-motion machine enough to linger over Windsor's nude back and boobs.

Both specials were produced by Geoffrey Owen-Taylor. The second was an hour-long live variety show. As well as introducing local artists, Sid featured in three sketches: as Mozart composing 'Three Blind Mice'; as a down-and-out beachcomber; and in the closing number as a mellow drunk in a nightclub bar singing 'One for My Baby and One More for the Road'. The 'baby' who joined him for the last chorus was Valerie.

The Jameses were living in a serviced apartment in St Kilda, overlooking the Albert Park Lake and a short drive from the television studios in south Melbourne. Owen-Taylor recalls his month working with Sid as 'very easy-going'.

'I remember him as ever cheerful, helpful, always prompt, and a thorough gentleman to everyone from the studio junior to senior management,' adds Owen-Taylor. Sid only once lost his cool. An actress arrived late one morning for rehearsal. Sid exploded: 'Next time take a bloody taxi.'

However thin his temper had become – and whatever fantasies he was nurturing for Barbara Windsor – Sid's libido was as strong as ever, even with Valerie in tow. Outwardly, at any rate, Sid appears to have pursued his casual affairs without suffering the penalties that would normally befall the woman-iser. To their friends and fans Val possessed enormous strength and dignity. The problem lay with her husband. Sid clearly felt he had paid the price of responsibility and was now collecting the interest.

It was now more than twelve years since Ronnie Wolfe had

confronted him about his numerous affairs. Sid's attitude had remained constant. In one remarkable double-take, a member of the Melbourne production staff found himself persuaded to provide Sid with an alibi. When the man gently reminded Sid of his marriage, 'a look of childish bewilderment and adult defiance crept across his face'.

Echoing Wolfe's experience, the man, who rose to a senior post in Australian television, said: 'The problem was that Sid could not see what was wrong with cheating on his wife, whom I liked very much. As long as his wife and children were well taken care of Sid honestly believed he was doing no wrong.'

In October 1972 Sid was shooting a film version of *Bless This House*. Although its roots were embedded in the hit television series it could just as well have been an unofficial addition to the *Carry On* series. Diana Coupland remained the only star – as opposed to Terry Scott, June Whitfield, Peter Butterworth, Sally Geeson, Robin Askwith and Bill Maynard – who had not appeared in a *Carry On* production. In addition, the film was directed by Gerald Thomas and financed and distributed by Rank.

Before he would agree to take part in the film, Sid insisted on one cast change from the television series. Again, this reflected his perception of professionalism: Sid believed there was only one way for an actor or actress to deliver a polished, seamless performance – complete dedication. There were no shortcuts. No easy options. On several occasions during the early series of *Bless This House*, Sid had complained to producer William G. Stewart about Robin Stewart's apparent failure to learn his lines. Stewart, who played Sid's son Mike Abbott, had allegedly been caught out several times hiding his script behind a newspaper or book – an allegation he denied. Whatever the truth of the situation, there was only one result from such a clash of personalities: Stewart was replaced in the film by Robin Askwith.

Pinewood Studios was less than a fifteen-minute drive from Sid and Valerie's home at Iver. When the cast and crew of the latest *Carry On* were packed off to Brighton for some rare location shots, Sid decided it was time he made a play for Barbara Windsor.

Sid arranged for the studio limousine to collect the blonde actress before picking him up at Delavel Park. As Sid settled himself in the back of the car, Val leaned through the window and offered Windsor a barley sugar 'as if I was a little girl who might get travel sick'.

With his wife safely out of sight, Sid moved in on Windsor. They chatted about jewellery and spectacles – it was the first time Sid had noticed her wearing either. And then – as the car swung on to the A23 and headed south – Sid got down to business. The principal *Carry On* stars had already agreed to appear in a stage version of the hit cinema series. Only Barbara Windsor refused.

'I'm very disappointed,' Sid said. 'You're part of the team.'

'I know,' replied Windsor. 'But I'd still be the *Carry On* blonde, and I don't want to take her on stage.'

'It's very sad,' her travelling companion persisted. 'We need an attractive, young, funny woman, and you fit the bill.' Inside, Windsor – still childishly unaware of Sid's real motive – knew he was right. As the car pulled on to the forecourt of Brighton's Metropole Hotel her resolve finally collapsed and she agreed to join the show. 'Great,' said Sid. 'Let's have a glass of champagne in my room to celebrate.'

Windsor adored a good glass of champers, 'so I saw no harm in spending an hour or two with him before dinner,' she later admitted.

As Sid was pouring the first glass of bubbly the telephone rang. 'Oh, hello, Val.' A look of deep panic swept the actor's face. He shook his head and put a silencing finger to his lips.

Windsor was puzzled and angry and demanded an explanation. 'That was Val,' offered Sid. 'She wouldn't like it if she knew you were here.'

'Why not?' Windsor snapped back. 'You invited me for a drink.'

'Well, that's the way Val is,' said Sid. 'It's best for her not to know.'

189

CHAPTER ELEVEN

The inkling of Sid's infatuation with Barbara Windsor had been there for some time. Windsor's dizzy naivety had led her to misread all the signs. 'I thought he just wanted to give me one – wallop!' she admitted.

It was ironic that just as Sid was about to embark on the most public affair of his life, he should decide to shed his image as a lecherous old man chasing dolly birds. Peter Rogers and Gerald Thomas had been under pressure for some time to drop Sid James as a *Carry On* regular. Thomas, in particular, was reluctant to do so. Not only was the actor a close personal friend, but he knew that Sid was still a major box-office attraction. To his surprise Sid himself suggested that *Carry On Dick* – to be filmed during the run of a planned *Carry On* stage show – should be his last.

Sid's main concern, at least openly, was that of over-exposure. He had already appeared in eighteen *Carry On* films. His comedy series, *Bless This House*, was still popular with television audiences. The public, he reasoned, could only take so much Sid James.

In private, Sid was acutely aware of changing public taste and his own image among younger fans. It was for the same reason that six years earlier he had refused to make a third series of *Two in Clover*. For Sid, and a growing percentage of the British public, there was something slightly grubby about a battered and wrinkled man in his sixties chasing semi-clad women less than half his age. As Jack Douglas put it, 'There comes a time in every man's life when he can no longer lech without being labelled a dirty old so-and-so.'

Carry On London opened at the Victoria Palace on 4 October 1973. It would prove a punishing run, even for those members of the cast who had not survived a major coronary. In a supreme act of irony Theatreprint, which had produced the *Carry On London* programmes, decided to place pictures of Sid and Barbara Windsor together across a double-page spread. The four other stars were Kenneth Connor, Bernard Bresslaw, Peter Butterworth and Jack Douglas whose brother, Bill Roberton, was also the show's comedy director.

In direct contrast to the austerity of the *Carry On* films, nothing was stinted to make *London* a lavish success. It was, at the time, the costliest show produced in England. The costume budget alone ran to over £50,000.

Linked by various song and dance numbers, including a tribute to the Royal Standard Music Hall which had once stood on the site, the show was based around three full-cast *Carry On* sketches: 'Emergency Ward 99 and a Bit' echoed the four medical films; 'Be Prepared', in which Sid played the scoutmaster, was about camping; and in 'Cleopatra's Boudoir' Sid swapped his film role of Mark Antony for that of Caesar.

Three weeks after *Carry On London* opened, Sid asked Jack Douglas to call into his dressing room for a drink. As the two chatted, Sid suddenly confessed that he had pulled every string he could to get Douglas dropped from the cast.

'I didn't want you in this show,' he told Douglas. 'I tried to get you out because you ad lib and I don't.'

As ever, Kenneth Williams recorded an acerbic comment on the show, which he did not get around to seeing until June the following year. 'It was like watching human beings forced into a pigsty and desperately trying to make light of their plight,' he wrote in his diary. 'The show is a pathetic rag-bag of end-of-the-pier and would-be Cochran-type revue with glamour girls and chorus boys. Perhaps the saddest thing is the audience. At the end Sid James came forward and said, "We're gonna do the whole bloody thing all over again!" and they cried out approvingly. When he had the temerity to ask, "Did you enjoy it?" they shouted "Yes!" '

Within days of the opening curtain, Sid's determination to seduce Windsor went into overdrive: from primitive lust to 'gut-tugging' love.

Windsor – whom Sid had nicknamed 'Tiger' – had so far ignored her co-star's lascivious remarks and wandering hands. 'I didn't mind,' she admitted recently in her second autobiography, *All of Me*. 'I thought, that's no big deal. I'll let him get away with that if it keeps him happy.' The puppy–dog loyalty and promises of love she found harder to ignore.

The more Windsor – twenty-four years younger than Sid and still married to gangster Ronnie Knight – rejected Sid's advances, the more jealous he became. 'It was terrible. It was hell,' she admits with hindsight. 'It's my nature to care about my leading man. It matters that we get on well. Sid stupidly mistook my genuine professional interest in his well–being for a definite come on.'

Sid showered Windsor with roses and expensive jewellery. When she refused to accept jewels, Sid insisted he would leave them to her in his will. In desperation Windsor confided in her husband, Ronnie Knight. He advised her to be 'kind but firm'. Just to make sure, he also arranged for the message to be delivered to the Jameses' Buckinghamshire home. When Sid and Valerie returned one night, they found Delavel Park had been broken into. Nothing had been stolen or disturbed – an axe was just embedded in the lounge floor.

To make matters worse, Windsor had, in many ways, substituted Sid for her own father. Her parents had divorced when she was sixteen. 'In many ways Sid had taken the place of the longed-for father figure I desperately missed,' admitted Windsor.

Between shows she would slip into his dressing room, cuddle up in a chair beside him and pour out her heart. 'At times like this I felt warm and secure in his company. I had no wish to hurt him, merely to stamp on his ardour.' But

Sid's love had turned to an undisguised passion. He not only wanted to please his co-star, he wanted to possess her. During one performance, as Windsor lifted her dress to make an entrance, Bernard Bresslaw offered his arm to support her. Sid went mad. 'Don't touch her,' he stormed. 'Get your hands off her.'

Sid haunted the corridor outside Windsor's dressing room and refused to leave the wings whenever she was performing. Innocent conversations with other cast members became whispered intrigue. Friendly gestures became threats. Laughter turned to silence. Sid's jealousy was as overpowering as it was destructive.

Jack Douglas, another of the *London* stars, blames himself for Barbara Windsor's eventual affair with Sid. The cast had been asked to appear on Pete Murray's *Open House* radio programme. The live broadcast would come direct from Victoria Palace. Because the show was scheduled for 8.30 in the morning, Douglas persuaded the BBC to pay for overnight hotel accommodation. Sid insisted on taking Windsor out to dinner, and she reluctantly agreed. When they returned to the Royal Lancaster Hotel they separated, but Sid promised to call at her bedroom later.

More than an hour later Sid had still not arrived. The telephone rang. 'I'm sorry to keep you waiting,' Sid apologised. 'I had to ring Val and then wait for her to ring me back.' When he eventually arrived he apologised again – this time for being 'too old' for Windsor. Lying naked and about to make love, he told her, 'I wish you'd seen me years ago.'

In her autobiography, Windsor describes her first night of passion with Sid. 'I just wanted to get it over with,' she says. 'It'll get it out of his system, I told myself. Don't get me wrong – I liked Sid, but I never fancied him.'

The affair gathered pace. Windsor arranged for them to meet in a flat belonging to her hairdresser, and which she had used for her affair with Maurice Gibb. And Sid finally confessed to Michael Sullivan that he was willing to leave Valerie and live with Windsor. 'I really believe he was madly in love with Barbara,' Sullivan said. He attempted to warn his client of the damage press speculation about the affair would do to his career. Sid replied, 'I don't care, Mick. To hell with them. I love the woman and I'm doing what I want to do.'

Windsor confesses: 'Sid put an awful pressure on the cast. Working with him while conducting an affair was awful. It was very hard. It wasn't a nice time for me.'

Whenever Windsor stopped to speak to Kenneth Connor or Bernard Bresslaw – both long-time friends – Sid would make a point of breaking in and breaking up the chat. 'You could hear people whispering, "Oh God, here he comes again." '

In the privacy of the dressing room Windsor would fight back, berating Sid for his unreasonable behaviour and overpowering jealousy. Sid would cry uncontrollably and plead for a second chance. The next day another bouquet of flowers would be delivered to Barbara Windsor's dressing room.

The vicious circle continued to spin dangerously out of control. At a London Hilton charity dinner Sid lashed out to 'protect' his lover, within earshot of his own wife and Windsor's husband.

On the dance floor Windsor and Ronnie Knight were energetically dancing, watched from a front row table by the Jameses. A man at a nearby table, obviously enjoying the performance, shouted, 'Go on, Barbara. Jiggle them about.'

Sid's face turned ashen and angry. 'Don't you dare say anything like that again,' he spat at the man, 'or you'll have me to answer to.'

In many ways, *Carry On Dick* marked the end of an era. It had already been decided that Sid's dual role as a vicar and as highwayman Dick Turpin should be his last. Every film or television special Sid had made since 1966 – with the exception of the *Bless This House* spin-off – had been a *Carry On*. Scriptwriter Talbot Rothwell was bowing out after twenty consecutive screenplays. There was also some discussion about how long Barbara Windsor, approaching her late thirties, could convincingly portray mini-skirted dolly birds. *Carry On Dick* would also be her last.

Rumours about Sid's antics at the Victoria Palace soon swept through the Pinewood lot. Gerald Thomas, a dedicated family man and loyal to Valerie, was shocked by what he saw and heard. In one scene, Windsor had to pretend to seduce Sid. Spending almost every hour of the day and night with her leading man, she could not bring herself to vamp Sid in front of the camera crew. Thomas was getting irritated by the delay to his tight schedule. In desperation, Windsor decided the only thing was to get the scene over as quickly as possible.

Sid had other ideas. He wanted to play it for real. 'It was ghastly,' Windsor recalls. 'I felt sick and degraded.' She eventually fled the set in tears. Thomas, aware of his friend's outrageous behaviour, took Sid aside and demanded an apology. Sid responded by claiming his marriage to Valerie was all but over.

Windsor decided the only solution was to break with Sid – and fast. When her six-month contract for *Carry On London* expired in March, she would quit the show. In the meantime, she attempted to keep out of Sid's way. Peter Rogers eventually persuaded her to stay.

Sensing the affair might be cooling off, Sid became paranoid at the thought of losing his latest lover. Whenever Windsor was on stage she would catch sight of Sid watching her from the wings. When she complained and fought back, Sid would dash up two flights of stairs and watch her, breathless, from the balcony.

One day Windsor arrived late at the theatre from a hair appointment. Sid was pacing the pavement outside, watch in hand. How dare he come the heavy with me? thought Windsor. 'I swept out of the taxi, straight past him and through the stage door without a glance. On stage that night I refused even to look at him. By the last act he had tears in his eyes.'

As the final curtain fell Windsor raced for her dressing

room. The door burst open. 'How can you be so cruel?' Sid demanded.

'It's very plain,' said Windsor. 'I'm bad for you. It's better for both of us if I go.'

To her dismay Sid burst into tears. 'If you leave, then I'll go as well,' he sobbed, falling to his knees. 'Don't you understand I love you? I want to marry you.'

Windsor was shocked but not surprised. 'Blimey, Sid, lay off. When will you get it into your skull that I'm not in love with you? I never want to marry you.'

Valerie was spending more and more time in the south of France. On the rare public occasions she was forced to confront her husband's lover she played it cool and dignified. 'How much Val knew or wanted to know I was never quite sure,' admits Windsor in *All of Me*. 'Though I had a suspicion she was well aware of it.'

In the privacy of Delavel Park there were bitter rows; slamming doors. A quarter of a century later Valerie can still only bring herself to refer to Barbara Windsor as 'That Woman', but at the time it is quite possible she sensed her husband's latest fling would snuff itself out and that Sid would not be able to survive – practically or emotionally – without her.

Wisely Valerie kept her distance. While his wife was in France Sid rented a small apartment in Dolphin Square, an exclusive block of flats in Pimlico, just down Vauxhall Bridge Road from the Victoria Palace. He justified his extended stay in London by telling Valerie his back was too painful for him to drive home each night to Buckinghamshire.

In the domesticated atmosphere of the flat Windsor began to weaken. 'I began to think I was in love with him,' she once said. 'Sid was so kind to me; he made me feel good. He told me he had ten good years left and that he'd like to spend them with me.' Sex with Sid was always highly explicit and satisfying.

During his run in *Guys and Dolls* a curtain had crashed on to Sid, damaging his spine. Emergency hospital treatment allowed him to continue with the West End show, but Sid remained in agony for more than twenty years.

Throughout the run of *Carry On London* the pain became progressively worse. Sid was irritable and easily annoyed. When the analgesics he had been prescribed failed to take effect, his face became drawn and turned the colour of yellow candlewax, and he walked with a slight limp.

Routines in the show were trimmed to take the pressure off Sid's back. Between sketches he would sit in his dressing room or, when Barbara Windsor was on stage, watch her from a chair in the wings. When it was suggested a sketch in which Sid threw Windsor over his shoulder was cut he reacted angrily. As the show entered its final week Sid became even more distraught at the thought of losing daily contact with his lover. He was in a 'terrible state' claims Windsor. For perhaps the first time in his life, Sid's professional career was being dominated by a new and fearful jealousy. 'I can't work. I can't go on.' He pleaded with Windsor.

In a desperate bid to prolong the affair, Sid claimed he had been advised by his specialist to take a long holiday in the sun. When Windsor refused to join him, Sid turned his back both on his lover and the show. While the last-night London audience was told he was too ill to appear, Sid was already on his way to southern Spain.

In the 1966 *Carry On* film *Don't Lose Your Head* there is a scene in which Sid stumbles upon the bedroom of the French actress Dany Robin. She instantly falls for Sid – alias Sir Rodney Ffing – and attempts to seduce him. It is a strangely prophetic episode which, eight years later, was about to have its sequel when Sid and Robin played out a second bedroom scene – this time with Sid doing the chasing.

Michael Sullivan had offered his client refuge at his home on the El Paridiso golf course near Marbella, where he lived with his fifth wife, Dany Robin. The agent was already negotiating a deal to transfer the hit Spanish television series *3–2–1* to Britain. Two days after Sid's arrival Sullivan left for Barcelona. As he was about to leave the house Sid stopped him. 'Send a dozen roses to Barbara, will you, Mick? Put in the card and sign it "Romeo".'

That night Robin took Sid to a party at a friend's house nearby. As the evening wore on Sid appeared relaxed and confident, showing no signs of the back injury which had nearly crippled him in England. The pair returned home sometime after three in the morning. Sid kissed Robin goodnight and went to the guest room.

Robin went to the family bedroom and undressed. 'I was asleep when I heard this mumbling,' she recalls. 'I turned on to my side and there was Sid, kneeling at the side of my bed. I thought he was drunk and praying and had lost his way.'

As Robin sat up, by now fully awake, Sid smiled for a second and then asked, 'Come on, Dany, what about it?'

As Robin remembers, she 'was shocked but kept my temper'. Calmly she told Sid he must be out of his mind and ordered him to leave her alone. Very slowly Sid rose to his feet, dropped his head like a naughty schoolboy, and sheepishly walked from the room.

When the pair met a few hours later over the breakfast table they appeared equally embarrassed. Robin commented on the weather. Sid talked enthusiastically about swimming and golf. It was two hours before Sid attempted to apologise. 'I must have been drunk out of my skull,' he said. 'Please forgive me, and don't tell Mick. We've been friends for so long it would ruin everything.' Robin, who was slightly amused and flattered by the incident, promised she would never mention it again.

That second night Robin was woken again. This time she turned over to find Sid naked in bed beside her. 'Oh, come on, Dany . . .' Before Sid could finish, Robin had leaped from the bed and was ordering Sid out of the room.

Sullivan arrived home later that day. 'I'm sure that if I hadn't been there on the third night Sid would have tried again,' said Sullivan, although it was another six months before his wife admitted Sid's bungled attempts at adultery.

'There can be only two reactions to news of that sort,'

Sullivan said in his autobiography *There's No People Like Show People*. 'Either you want to kill a man, or you laugh. I laughed, and then began to wonder about the supreme egotism of the man who would be prepared to try again after such a rebuff and making such a fool of himself.'

To recoup some of the early expenses, Peter Rogers sold the television rights to *Carry On London* to ATV as part of a stage and film deal. The entire Victoria Palace show was recorded. Edited highlights were then combined with film clips as a one-hour special and broadcast on 24 October 1973 as *What a Carry On*.

Television viewers were to get another dose of *Carry On* humour that year. With the huge success of the three *Carry On Christmas* specials, it was inevitable the idea of a complete made-for-television *Carry On* series should surface.

The task of getting the nine *Carry On* regulars who ultimately appeared in the two series to recreate the big screen sparkle was given to director Alan Tarrant. Filming started at Elstree Studios in the autumn of 1974. It was not long before Sid sensed things were not going right and pulled out.

By the time the fourth *Carry On Laughing* was networked on 25 January 1975 – the last in which Sid appears – the critics, if not the executives at ATV, were convinced the format was a flop. Surprisingly the ratings held up and a second series was completed and broadcast by the end of the year.

In Kenneth Eastaugh's *The Carry On Book*, Peter Rogers, the series' executive producer, admits, 'It was not what we set out to do. There were too many producers and other people involved, and although I had the power of veto I felt it could only make matters worse to use it.'

Sid was having better luck with *Bless This House*, by now into its fourth series. In 1974, *TV Times* readers voted him the Funniest Man on Television.

*   *   *

Barbara Windsor felt trapped and exhausted by her affair with Sid James. 'I was under his spell,' she admitted to herself. The passion had gone; she could see no future in it. Yet Sid had only to touch her – talk to her – and she would do anything he asked.

By Christmas 1973, Sid had returned to live at Iver. As a present he sent Windsor a diamond set in jet and surrounded by smaller stones. She telephoned Delavel Park on Christmas Day to thank him. To her dismay the actor asked Windsor to explain to Val why they should be together and promptly handed the telephone to his wife. For Windsor it was a final act of cowardice and betrayal – 'It made me even more determined to cut Sid out of my life.'

Sid was due to fly to Australia on 28 December. The day before, they met in London's Dorchester Hotel. Sid looked gaunt. Even standing was painful. He talked about his forthcoming tour and promised to sort things out as soon as he returned to England. When Windsor confessed the lingering affair was making her 'unhappy, very unhappy', Sid told her, 'If we are not going to get together I'll be dead within a year.'

As ever, union restrictions dictated that a high proportion of *The Mating Season*'s cast should be local actors and actresses. Among those auditioned by the J. C. Williamson Organisation was a young actress called Wendy Gilmore. 'I had no experience in playing comedy or farce,' she recalls. It soon became apparent to Sid that Gilmore also lacked any sense of timing. To solve the problem he devised a discreet – if not typical – form of direction.

One particularly funny scene, which demanded near perfect timing, involved Gilmore sitting on Sid's knee. After each laugh Sid would press his finger into Gilmore's leg, releasing it only when his instinct told him it was time for her next line. 'He never gave me the idea that I was inferior,' she says. 'It was simply an acting skill that I had not yet learned.'

By the end of the tour Gilmore's timing no longer needed a helping hand from Sid. In fact he was so impressed with her performance he suggested she travel to England to join *The Mating Season* for yet another run.

By February Barbara Windsor was also touring New Zealand and Australia. Once again Sid refused to let go. At each venue where Windsor was booked to perform *Carry On Barbara*, she would arrive to find a message or letter from Sid. Finally, on a Bank Holiday in Auckland, she sat down to write and tell Sid it was all over. 'I tried to make him understand how terribly wrong it was and how desperately unhappy his pestering was making me.' The letters, messages and gifts stopped.

Sid desperately needed a rest. The Australian tour of *The Mating Season* was over and he was exhausted. To delay his arrival in Britain, he decided to visit Phnom-Penh in Cambodia. While he was there he was introduced to a rich Cambodian businessman who appeared to know more about the *Carry On* series than many of those who had taken part.

After dinner the man suddenly announced: 'And now I will take you to the cinema.' It was the last place Sid wanted to go but, afraid of offending his host, he reluctantly agreed. When the entourage arrived at the cinema Sid discovered the man not only owned the theatre – but showed nothing but *Carry On* films twenty-four hours a day. Every seat in the house was taken. Sid was mobbed, not only by the cinema staff, but by the audience, who turned their backs on the film and scrambled over the seats to surround him.

Between the company's return to England and the opening of a ten-week summer season in Blackpool's Winter Gardens, the Jameses took a holiday in Acapulco. Sid returned from South America scratchy and bad tempered.

During his absence, the British cast of *The Mating Season* had been put through its paces by director Bill Roberton, the brother of *Carry On* star Jack Douglas. Playing opposite Sid, the leading lady would be Audrey Jeans. Plans were already under way to take the farce on a provincial tour early in the New Year.

Few friends had seen Sid so irritable. Michael Sullivan,

his agent, thought him 'overworked and overwrought'. Sid found fault with almost everything Roberton and the company had perfected. The entrances were not right; the timing was badly out; above all, most of the cast were not feeding his lines correctly. Sid's perfectionism was showing its raw edges.

Keith Morris, a young actor in his early twenties, joined the British cast for rehearsals during Sid's absence. He soon discovered how demanding – yet forgiving – Sid could be. 'It wasn't that Sid was greedy for laughs,' said Morris. 'He just wanted the whole thing right. He wanted the cast to perform to its best so that the entire show was perfection.'

The summer of 1975 was long and hot. The cast spent most days sunbathing or lying on the beach before returning for the sell-out evening performance. The matinées, with temperatures well into the eighties, were uncomfortable and distracting. Morris was playing Sid's son Mervyn. Three times he missed his cue – a sin, Morris learned to his cost, that Sid considered 'a capital offence'. As Morris day-dreamed in the wings, Sid ignored his stage name and shouted: 'Keith . . . Keith . . . get out here.' The audience loved it.

As the curtain fell, Morris awaited his reprimand. 'After he had been so tough on me in rehearsals I thought he was really going to lay into me,' Morris recalls. The ticking off was mild in comparison. As Sid turned away he smiled and said, 'You remind me of Bernie Bresslaw in the *Carry On* films . . . He was always off learning his Spanish when we needed him.'

Sid had not made a film for more than twelve months. The Australian tour of *The Mating Season* and its summer season had also kept him away from a television studio. The fifth series of *Bless This House* had ended in December 1974. The show had survived fifty-seven episodes and emerged as one of the country's longest-running TV comedies. Thames Television was making plans to revive the Abbott family; filming, for a new thirteen-part series, would begin in the autumn. The producer, as ever, would be William G. Stewart.

During the first week of March 1976, Sid gave an interview to a London-based journalist from the Johannesburg *Sunday Times*. It was one of the best acting performances of his life. Not once did Sid reveal the truth or the tragedy of his life. The words were what other people – what Val – wanted to hear. For the first time in public, Sid, then sixty-two, claimed he was planning for his retirement. 'I want to retire at sixty-five, like every other sane person, put my feet up and take it easy,' he said. 'I'll be able to give up show business without any trouble at all. It's not a drug – not for me. It's just a job and it's bloody hard work.'

Although Sid knew full well he would never live to see retirement, he did give an honest indication of the rift which had divided his family. 'What I want to do between now and my retirement is earn enough money so that my wife Valerie and my eighteen-year-old daughter Susan will be taken care of in the best possible way – financially.' Nowhere in the interview did he mention his son Stephen.

Finally came the biggest lie of all. Remembering his near-fatal heart attack in 1967, Sid alleged, 'I was asking for trouble. I was killing myself, and I was doing it for just one thing – money.' His illness may well have been 'a blessing in disguise' at the time. 'I was working far too hard and I don't intend to again.' The lesson soon wore off. Anyone who worked with Sid in the early 1970s, or saw his knockabout performances in *The Mating Season*, knew how little respect Sid paid to his doctor's repeated warning.

Michael Sullivan had watched his client's enthusiasm for work and sex slowly fade into a melancholic preoccupation with death. Sid James was dying of a broken heart. Life without Barbara Windsor was simply not worth living. 'He never got over Babs,' claims the agent. 'When he lost Babs he lost the will to live.'

One shocking confession convinced Sullivan that – if Sid did not have the courage to commit suicide – he was determined to drink and work himself to death. Sid was drinking at least a bottle of whisky a day. One minor benefit was that the alcohol dulled the pain in his back. One day Sid admitted, 'Mick, I want to die.'

At first Sullivan treated it as a joke: 'Come on, Sid, don't be ridiculous.'

'I want to die,' Sid persisted. 'I really wish it was all over.'

Sullivan is now convinced that Sid was deadly serious. 'The more I think about it the more I realise he was telling me the truth,' he confesses. 'At the end I think he actually worked at it.'

Whenever they met, Sullivan did his best to recall funny stories and jokes to make Sid laugh. Nothing worked. 'In the end he was just a sad, unhappy man,' he adds. 'He had success; he had money; he had everything anyone could wish for; but deep down, in his soul, he was painfully unhappy.'

Part of the problem, Sullivan still maintains, was Sid's failure to escape from a loveless marriage. 'There was no affection between Sid and Val,' claims Sullivan. 'He preferred to work than be at home with Val.'

Whatever the state of his client's marriage or mind, Michael Sullivan continued to cash in on Sid's apparently universal popularity. A sixth series of *Bless This House* was under way. The final programme would be screened just four days before the death of its star. Negotiations were also progressing for an hour-long Sid James television special. And Thames Television had signed to record the latest production of *The Mating Season* for transmission at Christmas.

Sid's earnings were reaching an all-time high. To save tax, Sullivan helped Sid and Valerie form Sidney James Productions (Jersey) Ltd. The new company financed the 1976 British tour of *The Mating Season*. When the company took to the road in March, Olga Lowe had joined the established cast.

There was a strange fatalism about the final weeks of Sid James's life. Some of his closest friends and associates sensed a change they had never witnessed before. 'I had never seen him so troubled,' recalls one colleague. 'It was almost as if Sid had lost the will to live.'

Relatives and out-of-touch friends found themselves drawn to making contact before it was too late. Sid's prediction to Barbara Windsor – that he would be dead within a year – and his confession to Michael Sullivan looked inevitable.

Reine James had not seen her father for years. Christmas and birthday cards had kept arriving; there was always the polite contact, but regular telephone calls had petered out not long after her marriage. One morning in early April 1976, Reine was gripped by a sudden feeling of impending loss. She immediately thought of her father. 'I just really felt that I had to see him,' she remembers. 'I felt I had to say goodbye, the feeling was that strong.'

Sid had just started his UK tour of *The Mating Season*. The show was booked at the Wimbledon Theatre, only a few miles from Reine's Thames Ditton home. When she arrived at the theatre she bought a ticket for the matinée and sat among the audience watching her father perform. 'I was sitting there thinking, What do I do? Do I go backstage or do I go home?' The urge was too strong. Reine turned her back on the performance and waited at the stage door for her father to come off stage.

'He came through the wings and saw me and there was this moment of stillness and we ran towards each other and had this huge, heart-stopping hug.'

Reine was shocked at her father's appearance and how small he seemed to have grown. In Sid's dressing room they chatted and shared a drink. Suddenly Sid announced: 'You'll have to go. I've got someone interviewing me in a minute.' The reunion was over. There were no promises of a second meeting. Reine was ushered out of her father's dressing room.

Sitting on the bus home, Reine attempted to make sense of the influence her absent father had had on her life. From her earliest years she had been sharing fame in the shadow of a comedy icon. She had, she admits, a 'very ambivalent time trying to establish my own identity as well as being his daughter. It was the only way I could be close to him – because everybody loved Sid James.

'It's difficult enough not having a father, but there is a strange sub-plot when your father is so famous. Not only famous, but loved.' Sid's physical absence was almost incidental. Every time Reine went to the cinema or switched on the television or opened a newspaper her father would be there. 'People would find out I was his daughter and tell me how much they loved him. But I wasn't allowed to love him.'

As the years went by and they drifted further apart, her father's new image – as the ideal husband and father in *Bless This House* – triggered an inner conflict. From Reine's perspective what people saw in *Bless This House* was 'a load of old hooey'.

'It was very, very difficult to come to terms with – especially in the later years of his life: the man as opposed to the image.'

There is a touch of bitterness in the way Reine sums up her father's life. 'I see him as a superb comedian and really fine actor who did, in some magical way, encapsulate something special for a generation of people. He had a really remarkable charisma. But he let me down badly and I can't forget that. I can forgive him – but I will never forget it.'

Within twenty-four hours Sid had been confronted by – and hurriedly dismissed – a second person from his past. This time it was Muff Evans. Unknown to Reine James and Evans, their separate reunions with Sid were eerily similar.

Since the 1950 break-up of Sid's second marriage, Evans had remained friends with Meg – one reason, she maintains, for Sid's increasing coolness towards her. They had not spoken for several years. 'Quite suddenly and for no reason I can explain,' Evans felt she must see Sid once more. 'It wasn't that I knew it would be the last time, I just sensed that I had to see him again – and quickly.'

Like Reine, Evans sat through *The Mating Season* at

Wimbledon before hurrying backstage. Sid threw his arms around her. 'God,' he said, 'we don't see enough of each other.' Evans, too, remembers how 'small and frail' Sid looked. 'He looked ill. Exhausted. He kept telling me over and over how "tired, so tired" he was.'

After just a few minutes chatting outside his dressing room Sid told her, 'I can't see you now, I've got a radio interview in a few minutes.'

Sid also made one last attempt to win back Barbara Windsor. Five months earlier he had sent a message through Jack Douglas, who lived next door to the Thames Television studio where Sid was recording *Bless This House*. 'He wants you to telephone him,' Douglas told her. This time Sid sent his former lover a telegram asking her to get in touch. Once again she refused to make contact. It was the last Windsor would hear from Sidney James.

From Wimbledon the production moved to Richmond, Surrey. In the audience for the Saturday night performance was a family friend who, forty-seven years earlier, had sat on the grass of a Halebron garden and watched Sid deliver his first, shy stage kiss.

In 1966, Sid had welcomed the woman and her sister backstage during an interval in the West End production of *The Solid Gold Cadillac*. 'He was alone in his dressing room and what little time he had during the break he gave to us,' she recalls. 'It was a wonderful gesture.' This time Sid would not even come out of his dressing room. 'We were told his wife was with him and they had to go on somewhere.'

On Monday, 26 April – Reine James's birthday – Sid and Valerie headed north for the start of a week-long run at the Empire Theatre in Sunderland.

EPILOGUE

Les Dawson walks on to the stage of Sunderland's Empire Theatre to open his show. He appears subdued, lacking his usual bubbly confidence. Several members of the audience – which includes a large party of schoolchildren – notice that the comic is shaking. He looks over his shoulder into the wings; he seems to be pushing the show along, eager for it to be over.

After the show, Dawson collects his things from his dressing room and leaves. He is strangely silent.

It is the last booking he accepts for the Empire Theatre. He flatly refuses to return. Pleas from his agent and theatre management to include Sunderland on future tours are curtly turned down.

Dawson is known throughout the entertainment profession as a highly intelligent and thoughtful individual. He is also a hard-headed businessman.

'Nothing would tempt me to return to that theatre,' he tells one close friend. 'And certainly not that dressing room. What I experienced in that dressing room will stay with me for the rest of my life.'

On 26 April 1976, only minutes before he died, the same dressing room had been occupied by Sid James.

APPENDIX A

Recorded film appearances
in chronological order

Year	Film	Role	Studio	Type
1947	Black Memory	Eddie Clinton	Ambassador	Crime
1947	The October Man	(Uncredited)	GFD/Two Cities	Thriller
1947	It Always Rains On Sunday	(Uncredited)	Ealing	Crime
1948	No Orchids for Miss Blandish	(Uncredited)	Renown	US Crime
1948	Night Beat	Nixon	BLPA	Crime
1948	Once a Jolly Swagman (US: Maniacs on Wheels)	Rowton	Pinewood/ Wessex	Drama
1948	The Small Back Room (US: Hour of Glory)	Knucksie	London Films	War
1949	Paper Orchid	Freddie Evans	Ganesh/ Columbia	Crime
1949	The Man in Black	Henry Clavering (Joint lead)	Exclusive	Crime
1949	Give Us This Day (US: Salt to the Devil)	Mundin	Plantagenet	US Drama
1950	Last Holiday	Joe Clarence	ABPC/ Watergate	Comedy
1950	The Lady Craved Excitement	Carlo	Exclusive	Comedy
1951	Tall of a Million (US: You Can't beat the Irish)	John C. Moody	British/AB Pathe	Comedy
1951	Lady Godiva Rides Again	Lew Beeson	British Lion	Comedy
1951	The Lavender Hill Mob	Lackery	Ealing	Comedy
1951	The Magic Box	A sergeant	Festival	Drama
1951	The Galloping Major	A bookie	British Lion/ Romulus	Comedy

1952	I Believe in You	Sgt Brodie	Ealing	Crime
1952	Emergency Call (US: Hundred Hour Hunt)	Danny Marks	Butchers/ Nettlefold	Drama
1952	Gift Horse (US: Glory at Sea)	Ned Hardy	British Lion/ Molton	War
1952	Cosh Boy (US: The Slasher)	Police Sgt	Independent/ Romulus	Crime
1952	Miss Robin Hood	Sidney	Group 3	Comedy
1952	Time Gentlemen Please	Eric Hale	Group 3	Comedy
1952	Father's Doing Fine	Taxi driver	Marble Arch/ ABP	Comedy
1952	Venetian Bird (US: The Assassin)	Bernardo	British Film Makers	Crime
1952	Tall Headlines	(Uncredited)	Raymond Stross/Grand National	Crime
1952	The Yellow Balloon	Barrow boy	ABP	Crime
1953	The Wedding of Lilli Marlene	Fenmore Hunt	Monarch	Musical
1953	Escape by Night	Gino Rossi	Tempean	Crime
1953	The Titfield Thunderbolt	Harry Hawkins	Ealing	Comedy
1953	The Square Ring	Adams	Ealing	Drama
1953	Will Any Gentleman?	Hobson	ABPC	Comedy
1953	The Weak and the Wicked (US: Young and Willing)	Sid Baden	Marble Arch/ ABPC	Crime
1953	Park Plaza 605 (US: Norman Conquest)	Supt Williams	Eros	Crime
1953	The Flanagan Boy (US: Bad Blonde)	Sharkey	Exclusive	Crime
1953	Is Your Honeymoon Really Necessary?	Hank Hamilton	Adelphi	Comedy
1953	The Malta Story	(Uncredited)	GFD/British Film Makers	War
1954	The Rainbow Jacket	Harry	Adelphi	Comedy
1954	The House Across the Lake (US: Heatwave)	Beverley Forest	AB Pathe	Crime
1954	Father Brown (US: The Detective)	Bert Parkinson	Columbia/ Facet	Crime

211

1954	Seagulls Over Sorrento (US: Crest of a Wave)	Charlie Badger	MGM	War
1954	The Crowded Day	A Watchman	Adelphi	Drama
1954	Orders are Orders	Ed Waggermeyer	Group 3	Comedy
1954	Aunt Clara	Honest Sid	London	Comedy
1954	For Better, For Worse	A foreman	ABC	Comedy
1954	The Belles of St Trinian's	Benny	London	Comedy
1954	The Frightened Bride (Reissue of Tall Headline)	(Uncredited)	Raymond Stross/Grand National	Crime
1955	Out of Clouds	A gambler	Ealing	Drama
1955	Joe Macbeth	Bankie	Columbia/ Frankovitch	US crime
1955	The Deep Blue Sea	A man	London/TCF	Drama
1955	A Kid for Two Farthings	Iceberg	London	Drama
1955	The Glass Cage (US: the Glass Tomb)	Tony Lewis	Exclusive/ Hammer	Crime
1955	A Yank in Ermine	Manager	Monarch	Comedy
1955	It's a Great Day	Henry Mason	Butcher	Comedy
1955	John and Julie	Mr Pritchett	Group 3	Comedy
1956	Ramsbottom Rides Again	Black Jake	British Lion/ Jack Hylton	Comedy
1956	The Extra Day	Barney West	British Lion/ W Fairchild	Drama
1956	Wicked as They Come	Frank Allen	Film Locations/ Columbia	Drama
1956	The Iron Petticoat	Paul	British Lion/ Independent	Comedy
1956	Dry Rot	Flash Harry	Rombus	Comedy
1956	Trapeze	Snake charmer	United Artists	Drama
1956	The Baby and the Battleship	(Uncredited)	British Lion	Comedy
1957	Quatermass II (US: Enemy from Space)	Jimmy Hall	Hammer/ Valguest	Sci-Fi
1957	Interpol (US: Pickup Alley)	Joe	Columbia	Crime
1957	The Smallest Show on Earth	Hog	British Lion	Comedy
1957	The Shiralee	Luke	Ealing/MGM	Drama
1957	Hell Drivers	Dusty	Rank/Aqua	Drama
1957	Campbell's Kingdom	A driver	Rank	Drama

1957	A King in New York	Johnson	Archway	Comedy
1957	The Story of Esther Costello (US: Golden Virgin)	Ryan	Romulus/ Columbia	Drama
1958	The Silent Enemy	CPO Thorpe	Romulus/ William Fairchild	Drama
1958	Another Time, Another Place	Jake Klein	Paramount/ Kaydor	Romance
1958	Next to No Time	Albert	British Lion/ Montpelier	Comedy
1958	The Man Inside	Franklin	Columbia/ Warwick	Crime
1958	I was Monty's Double	Porter	AB Pathe	War
1958	The Sheriff of Fractured Jaw	A drunk	TCF/ Daniel M Angel	Comedy
1958	Too Many Crooks	Sid	Rank	Comedy
1959	Make Mine a Million	Sid Gibson	British Lion	Comedy
1959	The 39 Steps	Perce	Rank	Thriller
1959	Upstairs and Downstairs	PC Edwards		Comedy
1959	Tommy the Toreador	Cadena	ABP	Comedy
1959	Desert Mice	Bert Bennett	Artna/ Welbeck/ Sidney Box	Comedy
1959	Idle on Parade (US: Idol on Parade)	Herbie	Columbia	Comedy
1960	Carry On Constable	Sgt Wilkins (Lead)	Anglo Amalgamated	Comedy
1960	Watch Your Stern	CPO Mundy	Anglo Amalgamated	Comedy
1960	And the Same to You	Sammy Gatt	Eros	Comedy
1960	The Pure Hell of St Trinian's	Alphonse O'Reilly	London Films	Comedy
1961	Double Bunk	Sid Randall	C M Pennington Richards	Comedy
1961	A Weekend with Lulu	Cafe patron	Hammer	Comedy
1961	The Green Helmet	Richie Launder	MGM	Drama
1961	What a Carve Up! (US: No Place Like Homicide)	Syd Butler	Pat Jackson/ Baker Berman	Comedy

1961	Raising the Wind (US: Roommates)	Sid	Anglo Amalgamated	Comedy
1961	What a Whopper!	Harry	Viscount	Comedy
1961	Carry On Regardless	Bert Handy	Anglo Amalgamated	Comedy
1962	We Joined The Navy	Sid James (As himself)	Dial/Daniel M Angel	Comedy
1962	Carry On Cruising	Cpt Crother (Lead)	Rank	Comedy
1963	Carry on Cabby	Charlie Hawkins	Anglo Amalgamated	Comedy
1964	The Beauty Jungle (US: Contest Girl)	Sid James (As himself)	Rank/ Val Guest	Comedy
1964	Carry on Cleo	Mark Anthony (Lead)	Anglo Amalgamated	Comedy
1964	Three Hats for Lisa	Sid Marks	7 Hills/ J Hambury	Musical
1964	Tokoloshe, The Evil Spirit			SA Drama
1965	The Big Job	George Brain (Lead)	Anglo Amalgamated	Comedy
1965	Carry on Cowboy	Rumpo Kid/Vicar (Lead)	Rank	Comedy
1966	Where The Bullets Fly	A mortician	Rank	Comedy
1966	Carry on: Don't Lose Your Head	Sir Rodney Ffing (Lead)	Rank	Comedy
1967	Carry on Doctor	Charlie Roper (Lead)	Rank	Comedy
1968	Carry on Up The Khyber	Sir Sidney Ruffdiamond (Lead)	Rank	Comedy
1969	Carry on Camping	Sid Boggle (Lead)	Rank	Comedy
1969	Carry on Again, Doctor	Gladstone Screwer (Lead)	Rank	Comedy
1969	Carry on Christmas (TV)	Mr Scrooge	Thames TV	Comedy
1969	Carry on Up the Jungle	Bill Boosey	Rank	Comedy
1969	Stop Exchange		Panorama Films	SA Comedy
1970	Carry on Loving	Sidney Bliss (Lead)	Rank	Comedy
1970	Carry on Henry	Henry VIII (Lead)	Rank	Comedy

1970	Carry on Long John (TV)		Thames TV	Comedy
1971	Carry on At Your Convenience	Sid Plumber (Lead)	Rank	Comedy
1972	Carry on Matron	Sid Carter (Lead)	Rank	Comedy
1972	Bless This House	Sid Abbott (Lead)	Rank	Comedy
1972	Carry on Abroad	Vic Flange (Lead)	Rank	Comedy
1973	Carry on Girls	Sid Fiddler (Lead)	Rank	Comedy
1973	Carry on Christmas (TV)	Various	Thames TV	Comedy
1974	Carry on Dick	Dick Turpin (Lead)	Rank	Comedy

Released after Sid James's death:

1978	That's Carry On	Various	Rank	Omnibus
1983	Carry On Laughing's Christmas Classics		Thames TV	Omnibus

INDEX

218